TAMING THE JUNGLE

TAMING THE JUNGLE

*The men who made
British Malaya*

PAT BARR

READERS UNION
Group of Book Clubs
Newton Abbot 1978

This book is dedicated to
The Winston Churchill Memorial Trust

Acknowledgments

I should like to express my deep gratitude to the Trustees of the Winston Churchill Memorial Trust who awarded me the Fellowship that made possible my stay in Malaysia for the purposes of research. I should also like to thank most sincerely the staff of the British Council in Kuala Lumpur who were so generous with their help and Christmas hospitality. My warmest gratitude also goes to the Directors and staff of Heinemann Educational Books (Asia) Ltd in Singapore, Kuala Lumpur and Hong Kong who have been so unfailingly kind and helpful in every possible way during all my travels.

On the home front, I should like to say how grateful I am to my dear friend Michel Block for his excellent translations from the French, and to David Farrer and Sophia Macindoe of Martin Secker & Warburg Ltd for their continuing and constructive enthusiasm for my work.

Pat Barr

Contents

List of Illustrations

Grateful acknowledgment is due to the Library of the Royal Commonwealth Society for permission to reproduce those illustrations marked * below

between pages 48 and 49

Clifford's house in Pahang★
Henry Ridley
Leonard Wray
Richard Winstedt
Frank Swettenham★
The Conference of 1903★

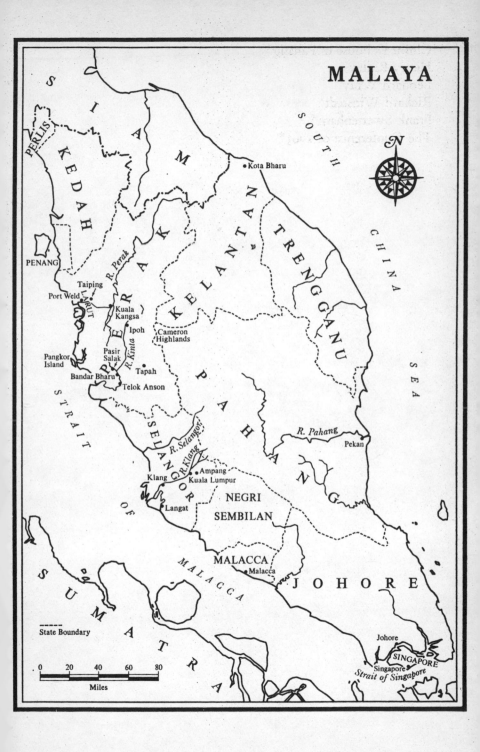

MALAYA

S I A M

PERLIS

KEDAH

PENANG

P E R A K

LARUT

Taiping
Port Weld
Kuala Kangsa
Ipoh
Pasir Salak
Pangkor Island
Bandar Bharu
Tapah
Telok Anson

R. Perak
R. Kinta

Cameron Highlands

K E L A N T A N

Kota Bharu

T R E N G G A N U

S O U T H   C H I N A   S E A

N

P A H A N G

R. Pahang
Pekan

SELANGOR
R. Selangor
R. Klang
Klang
Ampang
Kuala Lumpur
Langat

STRAIT   OF

NEGRI SEMBILAN

MALACCA
Malacca

J O H O R E

M A L A C C A

S U M A T R A

Johore
SINGAPORE
Singapore
Strait of Singapore

- - - - - State Boundary

0   20   40   60   80
Miles

1

Beginnings

It was early one November morning and the sun was already hot when I drove north on the main road from Kuala Lumpur, the capital of West Malaysia, in a hired white Vauxhall. I could afford to be there, doing that, because I had been awarded a Churchill Fellowship to research into, and write a book about, the British administration of the country in the last quarter of the nineteenth century – when Malaysia was called Malaya and several of its states were under British "protection".

The British first intervened directly in Malayan affairs in 1874, when they persuaded the Sultan of Perak, the largest of the west coast states, to accept a Resident, that is, a political adviser. Other west coast states, Selangor and Negri Sembilan, accepted Residents that same year and from then on British influence and control over the Malay States extended and deepened. The reasons for British intrusion at this time were economic and strategic, as were those of other trading peoples – the Arabs, the Bugis, the Portuguese, the Dutch – who had earlier established their presences in the area. For the Malayan Peninsula, where the monsoon systems of the Indian Ocean and the South China Sea converge, has, for centuries, been a natural meeting place of international commerce between India, Indonesia and China.

When the East India Company started to push its trading boundaries eastwards from India in the second half of the eighteenth century, a top priority was for a safe port-of-call between its main Indian base and Canton, which would also serve as a naval station to bolster British strength in the area vis-à-vis other, equally ambitious, European powers. In 1786, Francis Light of the East India Company, with three ships and a small garrison of troops, was allowed to take peaceful possession of the island of Penang, which he named Prince of Wales Island, the first British territorial acquisition in the Far East. Then in 1824 the valuable, long-established port of Malacca was ceded to Britain by the Dutch in exchange for the Sumatran port of Bencoolen, that had formerly been the headquarters of the Company's Indonesian trade.

More important than either of these in the longer run was the signing of a treaty in 1819 between one Stamford Raffles of the East India Company and the new Sultan of Johore which gave the Company the right to build a "factory" (i.e., a trading station) on the steamy, swampy little island of Singapore at the tip of the Malayan Peninsula. Within a few years Singapore was proving its potential and the volume of its trade soon exceeded that of the other two Company possessions, Penang and Malacca. So, in 1832, when the Company decided to unite their administrations, Singapore was chosen as the seat of the new Governor and the three ports became known as the Straits Settlements. Following the disaster of the Indian Mutiny, the Straits Settlements, like other of the Company's possessions, passed into the control of the India Office in 1858. But the powerful commercial establishment in Singapore much resented this subordination to distant Indian administration, and nine years later the Straits Settlements were constituted as a new Crown Colony, with its administrative headquarters in Singapore and under the overall control of the Colonial Office in London.

From then on, Britain's policy of not directly intervening in the political affairs of the Malay States was called into question increasingly by the merchant community of Singapore who wanted the extension of trading enterprise into the Peninsula. Moreover, from Singapore, perched precariously on the Peninsula's end, it looked as if there were two possible threats to the security of the Straits Settlements: that of encroachment from Siam, whose influence was paramount in the northern states, and that of the increasing violence within the nearby west coast states, whose internal affairs were in some disarray.

Conditions within the separate states, each a little world of its own, had seldom been peaceful for long in the past. The states were divided into a number of territorial units ruled over by chiefs who frequently warred among themselves. Outside and above this structure, each state had the symbolic authority of a royal family with a Sultan at the head, whose claim to the title was hereditary, though often in dispute. The Sultans maintained fairly lavish royal households and obtained the resources for their upkeep from revenues of their district and customs duties collected at the mouths of the large rivers – which were the main trading highways throughout the Peninsula.

During most of its recorded history the Peninsula's most valuable trading commodity had been tin. Until the nineteenth century the mining of tin was a Malay monopoly, and its production and export provided the sultans and the chief families with much of their wealth. But when the British settlements were established the tin industry gradually opened to individual enterprise and numbers of Chinese arrived on the scene to invest and trade in the precious metal. Soon they took over much of the management of the industry, introduced new, improved methods of production and began to import quantities of coolies, mostly from South China and Hong Kong, to work in the mines.

In the course of time, the Chinese – most of whom were young and male – had formed rival secret societies, as was their wont, and, in 1872, civil war broke out in the mining district of Larut, in Perak, where contending factions fought for control of the mines and the main river outlets. The Malays were also split among themselves over the division of tin-mining revenues, and the question of succession to the Perak Sultanate. Pirates, both Chinese and Malay, lurked among the swampy islands along the coast ready to pounce on trading vessels and, one way and another, the British could not rely on any strong central authority to impose the peaceful conditions which they demanded in order to exploit the commercial possibilities of the region more fully.

The resulting British "intervention" was the result of developments on the international scene as well as of local pressures, for the Colonial Office feared that, if Britain did not take the initiative to consolidate its position on the Peninsula and protect its South-East Asian trade routes, some other ambitious European power (probably France or Holland) would step in. Acting therefore on the time-honoured strategy of staking the first claim, and aware that the general tide of imperialistic expansion was on its side, the British Government sent the new Governor of the Straits Settlements, Sir Andrew Clarke, out to Singapore in 1873 with instructions to broach "limited interference in the affairs of the Malay States for the preservation of peace and security, the suppression of piracy and for the development of roads, schools, and police, through the appointment of a Political Agent or Resident for each State".

The road along which I drove had a made-in-Britain look about it, the surrounding countryside seeming very peaceful and secure in the soft gold light. I passed a bespattered rubber-tapper on a bicycle, an open stall or two strung with bunches of lush tropical fruits, a buffalo standing ankle-deep in a paddy field with a white cattle-egret picking ticks off his back, and a busload of chattering children on an excursion. They would be pupils from one of the modern-looking *sekola* which every village of any size possessed – together with a neat police station and a paved main street. The "roads, schools, and police", the British concepts of order and security, were undoubtedly still imposed, to some extent, upon this land – how much, I wondered, through the appointment of Residents?

Exactly how the Residents were expected to introduce these various reforms in the first place was not made clear however. Colonial Office instructions on the matter were cautious, suggesting that the main Residential functions were to communicate between the Malay States and the outside world and to protect British subjects engaged in trade. But Sir Andrew Clarke was renowned for taking firm and independent action without undue regard for the abstractions of principle and procedure, and his conviction of Britain's divine right to rule was similarly un-cluttered by doubt. The sentence of his to be most quoted by later historians was to the effect that "Malays, like every other rude Eastern nation, require to be treated much more like children and to be taught; and this especially in all matters of improvement, whether in the question of good government and organization or of material improvement . . ."

So Clarke considered that part of his new gubernatorial duties was the establishment of some kind of improving British presence in the most strategically valuable – and vulnerable – west coast states of the Peninsula. Within three months of his appointment he had organized a meeting with the native leaders of Perak to take place on Pangkor – a low-lying steamy islet in the Malacca Straits. The meeting, which began on 15th January 1874, was attended by the ruler (called the Mentri) of the troubled Larut district, by Raja Abdullah, one of the claimants to the disputed Perak Sultanate, by leaders of the warring Chinese factions, and by a British delegation from Singapore headed by Clarke himself. The results of the meeting were embodied in the Pangkor Engagement which confirmed the Mentri in his rule of Larut and recognized Abdullah as Sultan. In exchange for this British support, Abdullah agreed to "receive and provide a suitable residence for a British officer to be called Resident who shall be accredited to his Court and whose advice must be asked and acted upon on all questions other than those touching Malay Religion and Custom".

The word "must" was imperative enough, but in several other Articles relating to the Residential function there lurked a certain vagueness, for the British Government did not want, at that time, to take on any direct colonial responsibility for the Peninsula. In consequence, the Residents were not given direct powers of enforcement in the legislative or executive processes of the States concerned – which was to be the source of much contention later between the Straits Settlements and the Colonial Office as to how much authority and initiative they should be allowed to exert. In these ambiguous circumstances therefore, the Residents had the choice either of doing nothing much or of giving "advice" to the Malay Rulers and then creating the administrative machinery necessary to carry it out.

In spite of these insufficiencies, Clarke felt, with some justification, that he had made an excellent beginning in his planned extension of British influence in the area and, when he returned to Singapore, wrote to a friend that "all the people here say nothing has been done so complete and equal to it since Raffles' time". The first Residential appointment was actually made at Pangkor – where Captain Tristram Charles Sawyer Speedy was appointed to Larut as "Acting Assistant Resident" – a title which rightly suggested that the authorities were somewhat dubious about its holder's suitability. The first fully-fledged Resident, detailed to "give advice" to Sultan Abdullah of Perak, was James Wheeler Birch, Colonial Secretary in the Straits Settlements since 1870, who took up his new duties in November 1874. It was on his trail that I drove down a very minor, dusty and un-British-looking road which ran across the flat hot land parallel to the River Perak and threatened to dwindle into a mangrove swamp.

It did. I backed the car and returned to the last human beings I had seen – two Malays who sat at an open foodstall munching coconut cakes from banana leaves and drinking Coca-Cola. They looked at me curiously and one smiled. I said tentatively, "Pasir Salak?" which was the name of the village I wanted to reach. There were difficulties of communication and several other people, who lived in houses concealed in the nearby plantation, arrived to help. "The Malay," wrote a later, famous Resident, "is loyal ... hospitable, generous, extravagant, a gambler ... he has a strong sense of humour ..." Coconut cakes and bananas were pressed upon me and the fact that I wanted to reach Pasir Salak from there amused everyone. For I eventually understood that, though the village was on the same side of the River Perak as I was, the proper method of reaching it was by a better road on the opposite bank and across by boat.

It was too late in the day to retrace my route to any such extent and so, after much discussion, a skinny, sad-eyed man, wearing a faded cotton one-piece and carrying over his shoulder a dirty scrap of towelling which he frequently used to mop his face, was delegated to guide me to the village. On foot it would have been a simple, if somewhat tedious excursion; but the man obviously wanted a car-ride, so we got into the Vauxhall and bumped,

6

crawled, scratched and pitched along a jungle path which was really wide enough for only two wheels – one behind the other. A couple of workmen, carrying bundles of sugarcane, overtook us on their cycles; showers of sulphur-coloured butterflies danced about the thick walls of mottled-green vegetation on each side; the silence was broken only by the progress of my vehicle, which sounded like a bulldozer in that context, and the occasional startled squawk of a jungle bird in the highest tree-clumps. The car slithered to a halt twice in large wet holes and my "guide" grinned sympathetically at me each time, obviously thinking I was a rather poor driver – which I am not.

Pasir Salak proved to be a number of wood-and-thatch houses strung along the muddy sunny Perak River; it had a small domed mosque and a neat wooden school whose pupils had just finished for the day as we churned into the open grass space in front of it. They surrounded the car, beaming, squealing, poking their fingers in the windows. A grave-faced teacher wearing the usual black-velvet cap came up to me. "Birch?" I asked hesitantly. He nodded, and in good English suggested I follow him. He told me as we walked that the village had been knee-deep in flood-water the week before, when I could never have got through by car. "The right way is by boat – from the other side," he explained helpfully. I said, yes, I understood that now, but that one tended to make for the side of a river on which one's destination is actually located.

At the end of the village, half-overgrown by tall, sharp jungle grasses, was a Victorian granite memorial column with an inscription on it in Malay and English. About sixty of the children, who had followed us, fell solemnly silent as I produced a notebook and copied the inscription down; not because it had any rarity value, for its message is reproduced in several history books, but because it was, I felt, the expected thing for me to do, having obviously come from afar to see it.

Courteously, the teacher escorted me back to the car where my "guide" sat munching a bunch of mangosteens he had been given. The teacher and the children waved goodbye and, in my anxiety to return their salutations properly, I backed the car into a hidden ditch, thus confirming the guide's opinion of my driving incapacity. The children yelled with delight as they helped push the vehicle back on the path – which I managed to negotiate without further mishap back to the guide's house. He refused to take any tip for his services when we parted; presumably the car-ride had been pleasure enough.

As I bowled off towards the main road along the dirt track – which now seemed as smooth as a four-lane motorway compared to the path I had just left – I was singing to myself, with an absurd sense of mission accomplished and the clear idea of how and where my exploration into the "British Residency System in Nineteenth-Century Malaya" would begin.

2

"The bright sun of Western light"

Late on the night of 1st November 1875, three boats moved slowly up the wide, mud-coloured Perak River and moored in mid-stream, opposite the village of Pasir Salak. The first was a houseboat, mounted with a three-pounder gun, the other two were sampans, one carrying a mortar and ten sepoys, the other loaded with servants, spare boatmen and kitchen equipment. They were all painted white – an indication of their official status as belonging to the British Resident of the State of Perak, who was aboard the houseboat.

One of the other few Englishmen living there at that time described the Perak of 1875 as a "limitless expanse of jungle; miles upon miles of forest broken only by silver streaks, where one might, from a very high place, catch glimpses of some river. A few patches of lighter green showed where there were, or more probably had been, clearings. Excluding the single district of Larut, there was not a yard of road in the country and hardly a decent house; there was not even a bridle-path, only jungle tracks made by wild beasts and used by charcoal burners and a few pedestrians . . . The commerce of the country was by rivers; they were the highways and people would not leave them unless they were compelled to do so."

James Birch, the Resident of this untamed and uncharted domain, was a stringy man with a droopy moustache and a volatile temperament. He was fretful in spirit because he was the wrong man in the wrong job and secretly he suspected as much. Before he retired to his cabin that night he anxiously scanned the dense, rustling walls of vegetation on either side of the vessel.

Early the next morning the boats moved to the bank near the village; the sepoys and boatmen went ashore to cook their breakfast rice; Birch's only British companion, Lieutenant Abbott, went off to shoot snipe on the opposite side of the river. Alone on the boat, Birch began to consider how he would deal with the business of the day. Whatever he did would not be easy; since he had been appointed Resident exactly a year ago nothing in Malaya had been easy. He did not understand the country and he considered the Malay chiefs with whom he had to deal – and whose language he could not speak – to be untrustworthy and dissipated fellows who took a wilful delight in obstructing him in the performance of his duties. This pained but did not surprise him. As he had earlier explained to the Secretary of State, in his experience all Eastern peoples were "perfectly incapable of good government or even of maintaining order without guidance from some hand stronger than is ever to be found among themselves".

He was their strong hand and his duties were manifold: to restore peace between the warring factions in the State; to help and advise the chiefs in matters of general administration and the collection of revenue; to re-invigorate the production of tin; to relieve the condition of the peasantry, oppressed by an ancient system of debt-slavery. Birch had set about all this with clumsy, impatient diligence and had travelled hundreds of miles in his little white houseboat to tell the local chiefs and headmen what they must do under the new regime. "Have the Revenue collected at proper and stated places and by a fixed method", "Inaugurate a Registration System for boats and for people (with fines for non-compliance)", "Treat your household slaves less harshly and free the young girls among them" were among the many instructions he had issued during the previous months – regardless of the fact that he had neither the staff nor resources to ensure that they were carried out.

But the Perak Malays did not warm to peremptory plans for reform, and, as Birch had written in his April Report, they were "singularly averse to the doing of work even for hire, except the cultivation of their own lands or for their own purposes".

Rather, they watched the Resident's busy comings and goings with anger or amusement, likening him to a "Dutch sailor with nothing in his belly who came to Perak to collect the revenue of others", and interpreting his attempts to shelter runaway female slaves as a sure sign of hidden lust. The continuing lack of Malay cooperation and obedience had made Birch's position almost untenable, for, as Sir William Jervois (who had succeeded Sir Andrew Clarke as Governor of the Straits Settlements in May of that year) wrote, "When the Resident's advice is for the most part not followed, his powers of usefulness must obviously be restricted".

Recently, Birch's mounting frustration had often exploded into anger and contempt when he tried to cope with Abdullah, the young ruler who had been elevated to the Sultanate at Pangkor. Abdullah's claim to the title was not recognized by many of the other Perak chiefs and his control over the State was therefore incomplete and insecure. Moreover, Abdullah was considered by the British to be a most unsatisfactory character. His failings, which Jervois had listed in a dispatch to the Colonial Office, included the collection "of slave women, prostitutes and concubines, the smoking of opium, the levying of illegal taxes" and the hindering of the Resident's "endeavours to improve the condition of Perak". To deal with such a hopeless case, "one must be firm and even peremptory", Birch soon decided. And, "God help the country left to a man like that unadvised by sound counsellors! I very often despair when I think of him, but he will only be a puppet and, I believe, do all that one advises."

But Abdullah did not really relish the puppet role and he either ignored the Resident's suggestions for reform or took evasive action. "He talks sometimes a great deal of nonsense," Birch wrote in his journal, and, "Opium is become his bane again." Frequently, Abdullah simply failed to turn up when Birch arranged a meeting, explaining that "Perak custom was not to fix hours but to do it when it was lucky or convenient". To which Birch heavily replied that he too had a custom which was to fix an appointment and, if it was not kept, to go away –

which was just what Abdullah wanted anyway. But if this happened often Birch warned that the next British custom was "to take active steps and even to go to war, and we always fixed hours for beginning that event".

So much for the customs and beliefs of the man on the white houseboat, whose last fixed hour was almost upon him and whose very name is aptly reminiscent of the broom with which he hoped to sweep Malaya clean of its "corruption" and "chaos", of the switches with which he would have liked to chastise its "child-like" and "foolish" rulers.

The ruler with the most power along that stretch of river where the residential houseboat rested was Maharaja Lela, who had always been antagonistic to British intervention in the country. Though one of the State's eight major chiefs, he had not been present at the Pangkor Engagement, had never agreed with its terms and was a supporter of Ismail, one of the claimants to the throne whom the British had ignored. Lela did not conceal his dislike of the new order and stories were told later of the *mein berhautoo*, literally the "ghostly entertainments" during which Lela and his sympathisers appealed to the spirits of the forest and waters to get rid of Birch for them. That September, Lela had built a bamboo stockade round his house in Pasir Salak, and, when Birch sent a messenger telling him to pull it down, the Maharaja reportedly replied, "You can go back and tell Mr Birch to get all the troops he can from England and India and I will fight." A few months later it almost came to that.

Birch's first act that November morning was to send his interpreter, Mat Arshad, to Lela's defended house with a message that he wanted to see him. To which the Maharaja retorted, "Why should we go down to see him? This is not his country or village. It is ours." Lela added warningly that he had heard about the proclamations Birch had brought with him. The proclamations, issued by the Straits Settlements Government, stated that British officers in Perak were now to be known as Queen's Commissioners with powers to carry on the administration of the country in the name of the Sultan. Because the proclamations had already been posted in neighbouring districts, Lela was familiar

12

with their contents and had publicly stated that if anyone tried to post them in his village there would be trouble.

A man of Birch's stamp was not to be deterred by "native threats" however, and, after learning Lela's insubordinate reply, he told his interpreter to start posting the offending proclamations immediately. Then Birch stalked coolly along to the bath-house – a floating enclosure of logs and rattan moored at the river's edge – followed by a servant carrying his clothes and one Sikh sentry armed with a revolver.

As Arshad pasted the first proclamation on the wall of a Chinese shop, a restive crowd, some of them armed, gathered around him muttering angrily. Suddenly frightened, Arshad pleaded, "Don't pull them down. It's not the Koran. You can do what you like when we go away." The villagers looked at him scornfully, there was a jostle, a shove and the paper was ripped off the wall. "They've torn down the proclamation, sir," shouted Arshad, in English – and the man in the bath-house angrily ordered him to put up another one.

Birch continued his ablutions, standing on the slippery bath-house logs, his head occasionally visible over its walls because he was taller than the local population for whom it was built. But he did not see the eight men in the crowd who suddenly coalesced into a tight, purposeful group, armed with spears, krisses and muskets. They did not hesitate. As the interpreter was putting up the second copy of the proclamation they speared him and then rushed towards the bath-house.

At their approach, the prudent Sikh sentry leaped backwards into the river, holding his revolver high, and struck off for midstream; the men rammed their weapons over, in and through the flimsy bath-house walls. "I could see his head when the spears were thrust in and then I could not see him," the coxswain of the houseboat was to report at the trial of the assassins held in Singapore a year later. Blood sloshed between the floor-logs and into the muddy river. A few minutes later the naked white body rose briefly in the water and one of the men cut at it fiercely until it sank from sight. The eight men went to tell Maharaja Lela that the deed had been accomplished. At the trial, a witness was to

13

state that Lela "was the headman of the *kampong*. Whatever was done there was with his order."

There was no organized follow-through. Most of the sepoys accompanying the Resident managed to escape in small boats after a slight skirmish and Lieutenant Abbott also got away in a dug-out from the opposite shore. The men who had committed the crime received small shares of the booty looted from the house-boat and Lela kept the boat and guns himself for future use. For everyone realized, and Lela said, that what had happened was "only the beginning".

That night in Pasir Salak groups of men armed with spears and muskets gathered round watchfires whispering anxiously together, but, at one o'clock in the morning, another white boat with another white man aboard slipped very quietly and cautiously past them downstream, its Union Jack fluttering at the stern. If that man had been apprehended and slain there and then, as the villagers had intended, the story of Malaya's development for the next thirty years would have been somewhat different.

The man's name was Frank Athelstane Swettenham. He had been distributing more of the offending proclamations in the Kuala Kangsa area and was on his way back downstream to meet Birch when news of the murder reached him. Though only twenty-five years old, Swettenham had already been appointed Assistant Resident of neighbouring Selangor because of his considerable experience of Malayan affairs. Born into a family with a tradition of colonial administration, he had followed the expected pattern by joining the Malay Civil Service as a cadet. In January 1871 he had travelled to Singapore on a paddle-wheeled yacht called *Pluto*, one of the first two hundred ships to go through the Suez Canal, and, ever since, his life had been crammed with challenge and interest.

He had learned Malay quickly and, as an interpreter, had accompanied an early Governor of the Straits Settlements, Sir Harry Ord, on his first investigatory tours of the Native States; he had been singled out by the Singapore press as "no mere pen and paper official but one who knows how to use his tongue, his

14

arms and his legs"; he had been one of the first Englishmen to travel inland as far as the insignificant up-the-jungle tin-mining settlement of Kuala Lumpur; he had been present at Pangkor when the Engagement was signed and had helped translate it into Malay (a version later considered to be less precise than the English).

Swettenham had also been in one or two tight spots already while patrolling the coasts for pirates in H.M.'s gunboats and helping to destroy the stockades and arms dumps of the turbulent miners in the Larut district. But about the most nerve-racking and perilous episode of his entire career was on that night after Birch's assassination when he and his crew, knowing that the whole area was on the alert to get them, ran the gauntlet past Pasir Salak, because there was no other way to go. "We knew that the river shoaled here in the centre," he wrote later, "and that we must hug one bank or the other if we were to avoid being stranded. We chose the left where huge bonfires were blazing at short intervals with groups of armed men surrounding them. As we steered towards the bank a white fog came down and under its shelter we passed swiftly along, the light of the blazing logs, close though they were, shining vaguely through the dense white veil; while here and there a man's figure, of seemingly gigantic proportion, loomed out from the fire-lit haze."

At dawn, Swettenham and his crew reached the safety of Bandar Bharu, the village where Birch had his Residency and where they found Lieutenant Abbott, four blue jackets and most of the sepoys also safe and sound. The next day Birch's body was recovered from the river upstream and given a decent burial. "It was an impressive scene, more especially as it took place at a time of peril when no man felt that his life was safe," wrote one Major McNair of the Royal Engineers, who was among the first contingent of military hastily summoned from Penang to cope with the emergency. "The service was read by Mr Swettenham and due military honours were accorded to the fallen man, three volleys being fired by the Sikhs over his grave just as the sun was setting."

The next day it was decided to attack Pasir Salak forthwith,

15

"to avoid the appearance of indecision," as Swettenham put it. The small force – engineers, blue jackets, a few policemen – were "under poles", as the phrase went, by four a.m., landed three miles below the "rebellious village" and started "gaily enough" to walk up the river-bank, expecting no resistance. But Maharaja Lela had been quite busy in the interim. On the day after the assassination he had provided a huge feast of buffalo meat and rice for his villagers and then instructed them to build up new defences. At this juncture, most of the women, quietly despairing, bundled together their few possessions and slipped away into the protective jungle with their children. But the men stayed and worked as ordered, so that, when the British column emerged from a field of high corn about a mile from Pasir Salak, they were met with a fusillade of musketry fired from a strong protective stockade made of logs and bamboo. In the resulting confusion the sepoys fired on their own scouts, an officer was killed and several men wounded. The force beat a hasty retreat.

That was one of the very few reverses for the British in the so-called Perak War which was "held" as a formal act of retribution for what Swettenham describes as the murder "of an invited guest . . . with the knowledge and connivance of the Ruler whose hand gave the invitation and a number of his supporters who had agreed to a solemn Engagement which they had broken deliberately and with malice aforethought." The description is an early example of Swettenham's strong line in righteous indignation which buoyed him through many a dubious argument. To what extent Birch could truly be termed an "invited guest" and how much "malice aforethought" was involved in his assassination became a matter for later debate. At the time intervention seemed imperative – especially to the military men in the various Eastern cantonments who, having seen little action since the Indian Mutiny, were longing for something exciting to turn up.

Major McNair, most fervent apologist for the British over-reaction that followed, said that "Consequent upon the condition of Perak and the inflammable nature of the Malay character, the other States began to show strong symptoms of rising as if contingent upon the Perak outbreak, and further reinforcements being urgently needed, India was appealed to by telegram." In fact there was scarcely any sign of disturbance in the neighbouring States, but the military wheels had been set in motion and, as Sir Peter Benson Maxwell, an ex-Chief Justice of the Straits Settlements, astringently put it, "Up came the Bluffs and the Blue Jackets; the Goorkhas and the Artillery; and the Hong Kong troops and the Madras sappers and miners. The electric wire, let us hope, was to the fore and the engineers were surely not left behind."

All this, proudly wrote McNair, "must have made a great impression on the Malay chiefs of the power and promptitude of England when called upon to maintain the dignity of the Empire and avenge so cruel an insult as the present to her flag". The Malays would undoubtedly have been impressed by such a display had they actually witnessed it, but, as Sir Peter continues, "Everything seemed complete; and yet there was a want, an uncommon want – Where was the enemy? . . . Not more than twenty or thirty armed Malays were ever seen at any one time; and the whole number of men in arms in Perak throughout the so-called campaign probably did not exceed three hundred."

The man chiefly responsible for this classic case of forging sledge-hammers to crack nuts was Sir William Jervois who, wrote Sir Peter caustically, "was beset with the extraordinary idea that these Malays were a formidable people . . . The safety of our Colony seemed to him to depend on their being kept in order . . . and he fancied that a squabble among them in the depths of their forests was not only an evil exercise but a positive peril to our settlement . . ." So, having convinced himself that the whole Peninsula was in revolt, Jervois sent telegrams in all directions requesting massive quantities of men and arms.

Asked to supply no less than "two regiments of European infantry or 1,500 bayonets, fifty miles of telegraphic apparatus and a million cartridges", the Secretary of State, Lord Carnarvon, began to ponder if Jervois' continuing demands were not somewhat excessive "to punish what you originally termed an 'isolated outrage'". It was a time when "isolated outrages" were often used as sufficient reason for invasion and subsequent occupation

17

of foreign territories by various European powers. However, such a course did not accord with Britain's expansionist plans at that particular juncture, so Lord Carnarvon sent Jervois a stiff message to the effect that the troops posted to the Malay States "must not be employed for annexation or other political objects ... They are to be sent to inflict punishment for outrage and should be withdrawn as soon as it can be done with safety."

That message was sent on 25th November, by which time it was all over bar the shouting anyway. For less than a week after the minor British reverse near Pasir Salak, a contingent of police from Singapore had reached Bandar Bharu. They had attacked Pasir Salak, destroyed the Maharaja's stockades and then burned the village to the ground – most of its inhabitants having vanished long before – and Frank Swettenham had the satisfaction of retrieving his own dispatch-box from Birch's still-intact houseboat. The only tasks remaining for all those well-equipped forces from the far-flung imperial outposts were to try and capture Birch's killers and put down any further opposition.

Swettenham, who wanted to stay where any action was, acted as an advance scout for the China contingent from Hong Kong commanded by General Colborne and, in that capacity, had the satisfaction of exchanging a few shots with a small party of "dissident" Malays in a hut in the middle of a rice field who "withdrew when they saw the rest of the contingent approaching". For it had to be understood, wrote Major McNair, in laborious extenuation of the lack of an opposition, that "the 'jungle' is impassable, presenting as it does a dense green wall of vegetation on either side that cannot be penetrated on account of the manner in which the trees and undergrowth are matted and woven together by creepers and wiry rattan. In addition, there are thorns of the prickliest kind, one of which is known by the natives as 'tigers claws' from its hooked and formidable nature, while to crown or rather form the base of these difficulties, the soil is often one continuous marsh or swamp covered with vivid green moss which gives way beneath the travellers' feet." To which natural hindrances, he continued, was added the Malays' unsportsmanlike habit of felling trees and planting sharp-pointed bamboo stakes across the jungle paths as they retreated.

In consequence, when General Colborne's force, consisting of about 1,600 bayonets, with a battery and a half of Royal Artillery and a company of Bengal sappers, supported by a naval brigade, had stumbled and cursed and lugged their heavy weaponry through all that, and reached their ultimate objective, the chief village on the Kinta River, "the place was empty and deserted," Swettenham wrote. "Though there were signs that the last of the inhabitants had left but recently. I saw one good-sized wooden house, the roof of which had been pierced by a rocket . . . There was no other visible damage" – and in the absence of any living enemy on which to inflict any more, the expedition simply had to turn tail and struggle back to the Residency at Bandar Bharu. And that, concluded Swettenham, was the end of military operations in his district of Perak.

And in most other places, except for a few "mopping-up operations". On 4th February 1876, the Straits Settlements Government published a Gazette Extraordinary in the form of a Proclamation by "His Excellency, Sir William Drummond Jervois, Companion of the Most Honourable Order of the Bath, Knight Commander of the Most Distinguished Order of St Michael and St George, Colonel in the Corps of the Royal Engineers, Governor, Commander-in-Chief and Vice-Admiral of the Colony of the Straits Settlements . . . etc etc" to the effect that the British troops sent to Perak to "punish the murderers of the late Mr Birch" had "surmounted all obstacles" and destroyed all resistance. In these happy circumstances the people were urged to return to their houses and "live in peace among themselves", so that "anarchy and discord may cease".

In such a noble cause, wrote Major McNair at the conclusion of his book *Perak and the Malays*, poor Birch had died, "falling in the dawn of that day of progress for which he had so earnestly laboured when the bright sun of Western light was beginning to brighten the waving palms of this far distant forest land. Though his family will never cease to bewail his loss, there is a mournful satisfaction in knowing that he laid the foundations of a better government in Perak and that, as our influence over the Peninsula still further extends, his memory will ever be associated with the advance of civilization in this part of Her Majesty's domains . . ."

Frank Swettenham felt rather the same, saying in his brisk fashion that Birch's death "and the subsequent short occupation of the State by British troops did more to secure permanent tranquillity than ten or fifteen years of 'advice' by a British Resident could have done without it". Moreover, Swettenham himself had come out of the whole episode rather well. When it was all over he received a letter from Jervois congratulating him on his conduct throughout the assassination crisis and praising his "courage, ability and zeal". Swettenham was very ambitious and very able; he knew he was; it was gratifying to know that, as Jervois also wrote, his name had been most specially mentioned in a dispatch to the Secretary of State.

3

Terrible hot tedium

For several months after the cessation of open hostilities in the
Perak War, a more evenly matched, behind-the-scenes conflict
was fought between the Colonial Office and the Straits Settlements Government over the handling of Birch's assassination, its
causes and its implications for the future. Lord Carnarvon took
the view that earlier reports sent to him by the Straits Settlements
Government and the Residents must have been misleading and
misjudged in the light of later events because they had minimized
both the extent of Residential interference in each State's internal
affairs and the growing hostility of the inhabitants to such interference. Jervois was of the opinion however that the terms of the
Pangkor Engagement made it inevitable that more power would,
in practice, fall into a Resident's hands – for there was little point
in handing out sound, Western advice to the Rulers of the States
unless one then tried to set up the necessary legal and administrative machinery to carry it out. It was just unfortunate, he felt,
that the rulers and their subjects did not always accept with
alacrity innovations which were manifestly for their own good.

However, as Sir Robert Meade, Assistant Under-Secretary at
the Colonial Office and author of many trenchant and knowledgeable minutes on Malay affairs, put it to Carnarvon early in 1876,
"The treaty of Pangkor was based on the assumption that the
Residents were eagerly demanded and that their advice would
be readily sought and acted upon. If, therefore, in process of time
they should become the virtual rulers of the country, it is plain
from the whole previous correspondence that Sir Andrew Clarke
and the Straits Settlements *expected* that result would follow from

the influence they were represented as certain of acquiring, as the Sultan and Rajas were said to be only waiting to have the proper road pointed out to them, to adopt it."

But, as the fate of Birch forcibly demonstrated, the situation had not developed quite like that. So what was to be done next? In the first place, the original strategic and commercial reasons for British intervention in the Peninsula still obtained. As McNair bluntly put it, Malaya was "badly ruled, thinly inhabited, poorly cultivated and asking only for the direction of Western capitalists and the busy hands of the Chinese to make it one of the most productive under the sun". Should the British simply annex the Peninsula outright then? This course would have delighted the business community in Singapore and the British military, always eager for new strategic bases; but it would have involved the British Government in considerable expense without the prospect of much immediate return.

So perhaps it was best to blur the longer-term imperialistic implications of the Residential system for the time being and carry on business much as usual? After much delay – during which Carnarvon made it clear to Jervois that whatever decision was reached, the Colonial Office, and not the Straits Settlements, was ultimately going to make it – the last course was adopted. Carnarvon instructed Jervois in the summer of 1876 that "a modification of the previous arrangements will probably be enough for the present if combined with watchfulness and great caution on the part of the Government". In which case, Meade laconically minuted, in relation to the problematical state of Perak, "I should turn out Abdullah ... and put in Raja Yusuf or some other chief to be selected by the Governor. And I should govern the country in his name assisted by a mixed Malay Council." So that is more or less what they did.

Maharaja Lela and others involved in the assassination were finally apprehended, brought to trial, found guilty and hanged; Sultan Abdullah, whose complicity in the affair was proved, was exiled to the Seychelles; Raja Yusuf was appointed in his stead. There was also a shake-up of British personnel: one Mr Davidson, formerly Resident of Selangor, was sent to Perak in place of Birch – a hot seat from which he soon resigned; one Captain Bloomfield Douglas became the Selangor Resident; Captain Tristram Speedy was posted to Lower Perak – a move that was as declining as it sounds.

Had Speedy been a man of Swettenham's mould, his career might have rocketed upwards instead, for he was one of the mere handful of experienced candidates on the scene at the time of the Pangkor Engagement, when he was appointed Acting Assistant Resident of Larut. But Speedy was a born freelancer with more of a flair for independent pioneering than for everyday administration, and his penchant for picturesque extravagance perturbed his superiors. He was a large man with a fair beard who had spent several colourful years in Abyssinia and the Antipodes; he had been an officer in the Indian Army and a Police Superintendent in Penang, and had helped to quieten the pre-Pangkor disturbances among the Larut Chinese. Later, as Assistant Resident in that area, he had acted in his usual bold and individual fashion, simply "pushing on alone", as Swettenham said, without waiting for directives from headquarters. He had established a makeshift treasury, started a customs service for the fixing of tin prices, and opened a law court with himself as magistrate; anyone who did not approve of these innovations had his well-trained corps of Indian Police to contend with.

Speedy had also embarked on the development of Taiping, the capital of the district, and by the mid-1870s it was a busy settlement of about five thousand Chinese, with a few Klings from South India who acted mainly as drivers of gharries and bullock-carts and as lenders of money. Water courses and streets were laid out, the main one lined with a few public offices, and, on the central parade ground, Speedy's troops wheeled every morning in straight red lines. Attracted by these demonstrations of law-abiding security, people opened new enterprises: shops sold beer, wine and tinned meats imported from Singapore; there were brothels, barbers and bakers where the assistants filled their mouths with water and blew it over the kneaded dough to moisten it; there were blacksmiths, in front of whose sizzling anvils bullocks lay helpless with their legs tied together waiting

23

to be shod. By disarming the Chinese miners and "putting his foot down" on their troublesome secret societies, as he had been instructed, Speedy built up a reliable labour force; as prosperity increased, many of the local leaders developed considerable confidence in his abilities.

But for all that, Speedy was, his superiors decided, lazy, undisciplined, extravagant with public funds and his behaviour was much too eccentric and unpredictable. The Captain, Jervois complained to the Colonial Office, "has apparently a delight in dressing himself in a gorgeous leopard skin with a grand turban on his head, and still further exciting the curiosity of the natives by playing the bagpipes, an instrument on which he performs with much facility. If you have seen his elephantine frame you will be able to judge what figure he would present under such circumstances." Well, the man had had a penchant for turbans and leopard skins ever since his Abyssinian days and perhaps the locals liked him all the better for putting on such a colourful show. But the grey men in Whitehall no doubt imagined only too clearly the figure that Speedy thus presented – not at all suitable for his official position – and his days were numbered.

While the going was still good, Speedy devoted a great deal of time and money on the construction of a Residency of proper grandeur on his not inconsiderable salary of £1,500 per annum. It was built on a steep hill overlooking Taiping, with an immense verandah of expensively-planed woodwork. "A gorgeous retinue of Chinese attendants and a menagerie of elephants suitable to the dignity and comfort of an oriental nabob" were part of the household, according to one of his critics; from time to time, Speedy and his wife went on elephant-back excursions into the surrounding jungle (and further added to the native amazement by bathing together in the clear streams and taking siestas in large white tents which Mrs Speedy had made up on her specially imported sewing-machine). But this "lamentable want of economy" was the final straw, and in 1876 Captain Speedy was demoted to Lower Perak on half his former salary; soon after, as his superiors hoped, he resigned and left the Service.

Frank Swettenham, on the other hand, with his growing reputation for competence and the careful handling of revenue, was on the up and up, and, by the time Speedy resigned, he was in the Singapore government as Secretary for Malay Affairs. It was a post that enabled him to make use of the rare rice-roots experience of backwoods conditions which he had gained the hard way during his earlier assignment as Assistant Resident to the Sultan of Selangor. It was that appointment which had first marked him out from the ranks and it was reported somewhat tartly by the editor of the Singapore *Straits Times*, who considered Swettenham much too big for his young boots: "What then are we to think of the appointment of Mr Swettenham as Assistant Resident, and virtually Resident of Selangor? We disdain any wish to detract from the character or ability of Mr Swettenham, but here we have a cadet of four years' experience as a subordinate clerk in the Settlement raised at a bound and apparently considered fit to fill such a position . . ." Certainly the post offered promises for the future, but it was no sinecure, and, as Selangor's only white resident, Swettenham found the life fairly tough and lonely. But he was well used to this, having lost his mother when he was ten years old and spent a rather insecure and isolated childhood in the wilds of Scotland and Derbyshire where, he later wrote, he learned "self-confidence and a liking for aloneness".

So he had adapted himself to the rigours of Langat, a shabby riverine village on a swamp where the Sultan of Selangor chose to reside. Langat was renowned for the virulency of its mosquitoes and, to judge by the comments of Swettenham and other unwilling foreign residents there, its total want of charm. From his official "Residency", Swettenham looked out upon "a few score of blighted coconut palms with broken and drooping fronds like the plumes of a hearse returning from a disorderly wake; some disreputable and tumbledown huts; the dark brown waters of two deep and eddying streams and all the rest mud and rank brushwood. When the tide went down and the sun drew a pestilential vapour from the drying ooze, horrible loathsome crocodiles crawled up the slimy bank to bask in the noisome heat . . ."

The "Residency" which commanded this unlovely prospect

was a ramshackle wooden stockade which Swettenham shared with a guard of twenty policemen. Its mud floor was flooded at every high water, so Swettenham used to sleep atop the high log walls to keep dry – dry, that is, "except when it rained and that was on about half the nights in the year". In spite of an average daily temperature of 92 degrees, fires were kept constantly burning to keep the mosquitoes at bay and the "living-room" was always in a fog of wood-smoke.

Sultan Abdul Samad, whom Swettenham had been sent to "advise", was a small, amiable and unambitious man of enormous staying-power – he had retained the Sultanate for about half a century and was reputed to have killed ninety-nine men with his own hand in the course of it. A man of character and humour, he viewed the political manoeuverings of his heirs and hangers-on with a certain detachment and his life was one of "opium cum dignitate", according to Swettenham, who liked him – as most foreigners did. The Sultan also seemed to like Swettenham and wrote to the Straits Settlements Government to say that he was most obliged to them for sending him an officer who "is very clever, he is also very clever at gaining the hearts of Rajas with soft words, delicate and sweet so that all men rejoice in him as in the perfume of an opened flower". Swettenham must have found the terminology a little hard to live down, but was glad that recognition of his growing diplomatic talents should be passed on to higher quarters.

Keeping his posture thus sweet and low on the Langat scene, Swettenham wrote numerous reports about the dismal state of the local economy and the "oppression and cruelty which the chiefs heap on the long-suffering people" who "will not plant more than ten coconut trees because they know they wouldn't be allowed to enjoy them". He also tried gently chivvying the Sultan into putting his finances in order, fixing up a bank account in Singapore, getting some labour organized to build a road, a drainage system, a landing jetty. But Abdul Samad was too old to be hurried and, to judge from Swettenham's journal of this period, the young man spent most of his time waiting around in the rain and the mosquitoes for people to get down to business, or trailing hopefully after the ruler and his entourage, who would keep going off on hunts for tigers or turtle-eggs – which, like albino buffaloes and elephants' tusks, were royal perquisites.

Sometimes, in order "to live in peace and watch his own kettle boil", as the Malays put it, the Sultan appeared to acquiesce in everything. "He said he was prepared to do anything I told him," Swettenham reported at one point. "I told him I was very glad to hear him say so, as I felt sure it was the best thing he could do. I told him all I wanted was that he should come to Singapore. He said, very well, he was ready to go." But old Abdul was not really, for he knew if he went to Singapore he would end up by signing more of the white man's documents which he did not fully understand and agreeing to do a lot of things he did not want to bother about. So he did not go to Singapore and, in spite of Swettenham's sweetness, he was probably relieved when that busy young official was called away to assist the ill-fated Birch, and was then detained by the subsequent dramatic developments in Perak and then posted to Singapore himself instead.

But it was too much for Abdul Samad to hope that he would be left to "watch his own kettle" for long, and, in the summer of 1876, when the general move-around of officials took place, the British abolished the Resident status of Langat and sent instead a Collector and Magistrate, whose main duties were to organize revenue collection and judge minor offences in the surrounding district. The man first appointed to the post was James Innes, a mediocre administrator with a fatal capacity for speaking his mind to the wrong people at the wrong time, an overwrought, heavy-drinking, weak-willed man – but with a wife of unusual spirit and courage, who is the main reason why his name still features in historical footnotes.

Her name was Emily, and when the news of James' new posting came, she determined to go with him, a resolve only stiffened by an official in the Singapore government who told her that it was "perfectly impossible for an Englishwoman" to live at Langat. So she went, stuck it out and afterwards wrote a quaint, bitter, honest book about it called *The Chersonese with the Gilding Off* which gives an unusually vivid picture of the isolated tedium of British officials' daily lives in the Malayan interiors, at a time when communications with the outside world were intermittent and tenuous.

By the time Emily arrived, the "Residence" at Langat had been improved from the oft-flooded wooden stockade to what she terms "an ordinary Malay wigwam" of attap-thatch and wood, raised on poles four feet above the mud. There was a "biggish loft", which James used as a court-room, two bed-rooms, a store-room, and a passage that "served as a dining-room"; there were no verandahs or windows, so that when it rained they had either to close the shutters and sit in the dark or to leave them open and remain exposed to the elements. James preferred the latter, which meant that, during the frequent and violent storms, his "papers, ledgers, pens, inkstands, rulers and even the cane chairs and tables were sometimes blown out on the mud below". Fortunately, she continues, for she has a nice touch of irony, "the mud was so sticky and the rain so heavy that the papers never flew far, though sometimes they were reduced to a pulp".

Mud, clearly, was Langat's central feature: worms slithered through it; crocodiles (as Swettenham noted) basked on it; scavenger fowls, egrets, stone plovers pecked at it; mosquitoes whined above it; buffaloes, goats and children excreted in it; from the jungle trees nearby troops of grey monkeys sometimes waded in it seeking the small shrimps stranded by the tide; jumping fish leaped about and burrowed in it; egg and coconut shells, banana-skins, discarded fish-heads and the occasional magisterial paper adhered to its sticky surface.

The village's only path was also made of mud. It led through the bazaar, which, Emily wrote, consisted of several stalls where a few "squalid wares were displayed, hanging from strings or shut up in glass bottles on account of the ants", past three houses of some small pretension owned by the Chinese gambling and opium farmers, and Abdul Samad's residence, "a dilapidated wooden building". Then it narrowed, steepened, tailed off in four miles of flat swamp beyond which a hill, called Jugra, shimmered in the hot distance. The first time that the Inneses stood together at the end of that mud path looking at that hill, "we agreed aloud," Emily wrote, "that if we had to remain six months in this fearful place we must either leave the service or commit suicide."

In the event they did neither, but stayed there for four years during which Emily became intimately acquainted with every blue land-crab, scrap of bog myrtle and "slimy amphibian" that lived along that wretched path, and her husband somewhat perfunctorily performed his duties which she archly described as making sure that the Sultan "did not get into mischief" and warning him "that Queen Victoria did not approve of piracy, slavery, pawnbroking and other little failures to which he was addicted". Abdul Samad had abandoned piracy anyway because, Emily felt, he had found it easier and more profitable to "take the British government to his bosom"; his "other little failings" – opium smoking and cock-fighting – he did not give up and, on her restricted perambulations, she used often to come upon the wizened little man "seated astride a carpenter's bench or else squatting on the ground amid a crowd of dirty followers watching a cock-fight ... He was usually dressed in nothing but a very scanty little cotton kilt or a pair of still scantier bathing drawers." Nevertheless he could summon the requisite royal dignity when occasion demanded and, on his homage days, Emily records that he wore "a jacket of sprigged silk buttoned with diamonds over his kilt", and all his subjects, rajas included, crawled along the ground to kiss his skinny hand.

The Sultan was generous to a fault – every starving human waif, mangy cat, pariah dog found their way to his dwelling and he gave them food and shelter, as was the custom of the country. Indeed he disliked receiving too much money from his tin revenues because he was only the more pestered to give it away – which he did to such an extent that Swettenham acidly commented he was in danger of becoming "an occupational pauper", in spite of the generous living allowance granted him by the government. While Innes was at Langat he saw to it that some of the Sultan's funds were directed towards goodly supplies of champagne and claret imported from London and in due course

29

the Sultan also conveniently developed a taste for foreign-style linen and china. In due course too, the Inneses developed "not only a feeling of warm friendship but even a respect" for Abdul Samad, and it was apparently mutual for, when James was away along the coasts inspecting fishing-traps, tin-mines and police stations, the Sultan offered Emily a bodyguard of his own men to protect her. As she remarked however, it says much for the peaceful and civilized nature of the people that she always felt perfectly safe alone among them and neither she nor the property "were ever molested".

Even some small molestation might have been welcome to relieve the terrible hot tedium of the days. There was nowhere to go except along the mud path; there was nothing to do except take two or three baths a day to cool down, superintend the primitive preparations for the monotonous rice/egg/fish meals, mend the household linen and rush out every time she heard one of her hens cackling in order to secure the egg before it was stolen by one of the ditch-digging coolies. Emily became rather fond of her hens, strong and intelligent birds "but a generation or two removed from the wild jungle-fowl". Their "ruling passion was for laying in the most unsuitable place they could find". The pigeon-holes in James' desk were a favourite nest for depositing eggs and even rearing families; Emily also found eggs and chicks in her work-basket, pails, beds, hats and bookshelves.

But the company of the idiosyncratic hens was often preferable to that of her irritable and anxious husband or the villagers who just used to turn up at the house day after day. They squatted on the floor and watched her for hours, "as if they had taken root", filling the air with the smell of stale perspiration and rancid hair-oil. The women were the worst, Emily decided, for they knew nothing whatsoever of the taboos of "polite society" and "the first half dozen questions which each female visitor in Langat used to ask me would make an English reader's hair stand on end". (Probably the first two would be. Was her husband impotent? Was that why she had no children?)

The visitors were only dislodged by the approach of sunset, at which hour the notorious Langat mosquitoes "rose up in their thousands from the swamp with an audible hum like distant bees". To escape them, the Inneses took refuge in their "mosquito house, a sort of large square cage made of wooden bars with mosquito netting nailed to it ... The cage contained a couple of rattan lounges and a small table; on the latter we put our lamp and our books or work, while thousands of baffled insects of all kinds swarmed on the netting outside gazing into our Eden like so many Peris and thirsting for our blood." When they ventured forth to eat supper, insects of every sort came swarming in through the open doorways: "carpenter beetles buzzed in our soup, locusts whirred in our tumblers, hornets entangled themselves in our hair while crowds of unknown species lay about the table, more or less singed by the visits they had first paid to the candles." In short, the local fauna took the Innes' dwelling for their own: lizards snoozed in the wall crevices, stinging centipedes lurked in the bath-tub, frogs hopped occasionally on the sitting-room mats, scorpions curled under the bed.

And so the hazard-ridden, tedious days slid by each one exactly like the one before – the hour of sunrise, the increasing heat, the afternoon storms, the hour of sunset; yet the only interruptions were invariably unpleasant. Some pirates came prowling up-river once and lonely fishermen in huts along the banks were robbed and stabbed; there was a cholera outbreak and stinking corpses were left in nearby houses from which the inhabitants had fled in fear; sometimes, on especially dark and moonless nights, tigers prowled and roared so close to the house that the policeman on guard outside came hurrying upstairs into the sitting-room for safety. For tigers abounded in the area and every village had its ghastly story of "the low crouching horror with the cruel fangs" who pounced out of the jungle dark on some lonely, frail or sleeping victim.

The only other, and equally unwelcome, disruption of Emily's monotonous days was the roaring voice of Captain Bloomfield Douglas, the Resident of Selangor, whose official launch, the *Abdul Samad*, used to chug down-river unannounced on many a sleepy afternoon. Douglas, a florid middle-aged man, had pursued a footloose career on several of the imperial fringes. He had been a commander of James Brooke's schooner in Sarawak; a merchant naval officer; an administrator in West Australia; a police-magistrate in Singapore – a man who obviously felt himself born to command, but, to judge by his contemporaries' comments, conspicuously lacked the talent for so doing. He was bombastic, opinionated and pompous – soon after his appointment to the Resident's post in 1876 he applied unsuccessfully for the title of "Honorary Captain of the Royal Naval Reserve" in order not to appear as a "simple Mr among the natives". But he used the Captain's title anyway and cultivated a voice of command which, Emily noted caustically, "was pitched in tones that would have done admirably well for giving orders during a storm at sea and trying to drown the elements".

Whenever the sound of that voice and the launch's whistle reached Mrs Innes' ears she rushed down to the kitchen and ordered the cook's boy to go and catch two or three of her hens "to be held in readiness until we knew how many men the Resident had brought with him". The men, who came mainly to shoot snipe on the swamps behind Langat, might be "Scotch engineers of small coasting steamers, half-caste apothecaries or accountants etc or English policemen of the rough and ready sort". Though she secretly and strongly disapproved of such "ill-bred" assemblages, Douglas was the boss and Emily had no choice but to provide sustenance for them.

So, while the cook quickly killed and plucked the requisite number of fowls and the men went off for their shooting, Emily ransacked her store-room for pickles, tins of fruit, poor Australian wine – anything to make the inevitable chicken curry seem more palatable. Later, after consuming all she could offer, the men went steaming off in the yacht, usually taking every bird they had shot with them and leaving Emily to contemplate the depletion of her stores and the tedium of her future. For, as she wryly says, she learned from bitter experience "that the less you have to eat, the more you think about it, especially if you have nothing much else to think about".

The vessel which Douglas used was a travelling arsenal of gleaming rifles, bayonets, cutlasses and boarding pikes – because, beneath his swaggering bombast, there cowered a deep terror of the country. Douglas' Residency was situated in Klang, a village of about fifty weathered-thatch houses on the banks of the River Klang. The place had a neglected and dilapidated air – a rickety wharf, a tumbledown storage shed, and several of the houses with holes in large enough to throw a dog through, according to the American naturalist, William Hornaday, who visited it in 1877. "I suppose," he wrote in his dry American fashion, "that, like the man of Arkansas, when it rained they couldn't fix the roof and when it didn't rain they didn't need to."

What Douglas had built in Klang was indicative of his character: one white-painted public building which served as court-house and treasury; one jail enclosed by a high wall and containing several prisoners in irons, most of them Chinese; and one fort, a prominent building surrounded by guns mounted on grass embankments. Above the fort was a spacious bungalow where Douglas lived with his wife, "a gracious and dignified woman with a sweet but plaintive expression", according to another visitor, and his two daughters, one a semi-invalid, the other married to an Australian surveying engineer called Dominic Daly.

In front of the bungalow a British ensign hung limply from a flagstaff, and on its porch stood a large gong, at the sound of which, Douglas boasted, a hundred armed men would turn out to defend him in five minutes. The force was under the command of Harry Syers, a young soldier of unusual ability who had been released from the 10th Regiment to take the post. He lived in the fort where he superintended the police with diligent efficiency. His character, according to Hornaday, was "fit to do duty as the hero of a vigorous romance", for he was "big-hearted, fearless as a lion-tamer and tenacious". It was the Resident who was afraid and, to keep that fear at bay, he used frequently to drill Syers' men on the parade ground – an exercise for which his stentorian voice was admirably suited and which gave him an excellent chance to wear his full-dress uniform, its gold epaulettes and dress sword shining in the sun.

Procedures such as this gave the jittery despot the reassurance he needed for a task that would not have been easy for a much more able man. His predecessor, James Davidson, had made a short-term success of the job largely because he had long been a trusted friend and adviser of Tunku Kudin, the Sultan's Viceroy and a man who took an energetic interest in the reforming measures which the British proposed. Douglas, who did not understand the country or its language, had little hope of succeeding in a position which had to be maintained through the exercise of adroit diplomacy rather than crude force. He was unable to gain the confidence and cooperation of the Selangor chiefs and so totally antagonized Tunku Kudin that he soon resigned and left the State.

From then on Douglas' position worsened because he had to get on as best he might with Raja Muda, the strictly religious eldest son of old Abdul Samad, and with Raja Mahmood, an unsuccessful claimant to the Sultan's throne. Mahmood had been directed to take charge of the Sappang district under the supervision of James Innes but, like several of the young Malay nobility, refused to settle down and do just what his foreign "advisers" told him. The heavy-handed authoritarianism with which Douglas tried to cope with the situation is apparent in his own report of a reproof which he administered to the erring Raja: "The Resident told Raja Mahmood that it was impossible that the country under him would do any good or that he could induce settlement to come into the place while he was constantly away. There was no one to attend to these interests. It was like a ship without a Captain ... He reminded Raja Mahmood of the many promises of reform which had never been carried out ... However he was willing to forget all that, if Raja Mahmood would now turn over a new leaf and settle down at Sappang ..."

A few months previously, Douglas and Innes had made the mistake of withholding Mahmood's allowance on account of his unsatisfactory behaviour, and Swettenham, who was Mahmood's friend, was furious at the peremptory decision and demanded that it be rescinded immediately. Douglas had no choice but to comply – another cross he had to bear was the close surveillance of the indefatigable, ambitious, locally-knowledgeable and young Assistant Secretary for Native Affairs. For Swettenham was secretly convinced that he would make a much more effective Resident of Selangor than the present not very sagacious incumbent, who persisted in treating the local rajas like a bunch of semi-delinquent schoolboys.

That same year, 1878, Douglas, who was not a man to learn from past mistakes, again roused the furious displeasure of the Singapore government by staging a ceremony of reprimand on board H.M. vessel *Fly*. Before an especially assembled audience of the ship's crew and the neighbouring villagers he "administered reproof and caution from the quarter deck" to one Raja Etam for maladministration and the illegal harbouring of a female slave. He concluded by saying that the Raja's misdemeanours would be forgiven providing he started to rule "in accordance with the law, the commands of the Sultan and the advice of the Collector and Magistrate, given in my name . . ." When Swettenham heard about it, he sent a biting letter to Douglas pointing out that Her Majesty's ships were not to be used to "convey the Resident about on semi-political missions" and that the British policy of "gradual advancement" would not be helped by such high-handed behaviour.

But, for the time being, Douglas was allowed to continue on his erratic and ill-judged course, partly because of the lack of a more experienced and capable man to replace him. In the mornings, Klang rang with the sound of his thunderous voice and the clank of police-force weaponry; in the afternoons, the Resident's wife looked out plaintively from her verandah over the green waves of jungle to the blueish hills shimmering in the heat beyond, or, more hopefully, towards the post office in the street to see if a flag had been raised to signify the arrival of mail from Singapore. Towards sunset, the little port took on a soft beauty, "with palms against a golden sky, pink clouds, a pink river and a balm-breathing air, just strong enough to lift the heavy-scented flowers which make the evenings delicious . . ."

However, that was written by a privileged lady traveller from England called Isabella Bird, who stayed with the Douglases in 1879 – one free to move on to the next Residency when she chose and beset by none of those harassments and secret fears that afflicted Douglas. She was a perceptive judge of character and she greatly disliked Douglas. In a later private letter, written after her return home, she claimed that his "mis-government of the State was gross and brutal. I saw scenes in which the Resident was the chief actor of the most brutal description and heard more than I saw. It was rule of fraud, hypocrisy and violence . . ."

That being the case, and unable to do anything about it, Isabella Bird was very relieved to board the Residential yacht which carried her back to the comparatively civilized Penang. There, aboard the P. & O. steamer *Peking* which was anchored in the harbour, she was introduced to Mr Hugh Low, the Resident of Perak. There could have been no greater contrast than the ways in which Low and Douglas went about their essentially similar tasks – as Miss Bird soon discovered for herself.

4

Fiction and Function

Hugh Low was a man of a totally different stamp from Bloomfield Douglas, being unafraid, tolerant, unpretentious and with a considerable understanding of Malay psychology and language. Low had lived in the East more or less continuously since 1843 when, at the age of nineteen, he was sent to Borneo by his father, a self-made Scot and a horticulturist with a special interest in tropical plants. Low inherited his father's enthusiasm; he loved growing things and became an expert on the flora and fauna of the region. While in Borneo, he came under the influence of James Brooke, a man for whom he had a lifelong respect. Brooke's idea of showing "proper deference" to the opinions of the native chiefs, because it "satisfies them and strengthens you", appealed to Low's undoctrinaire temperament and, from the first, he tried to put Brooke's philosophy into practice in Perak.

But between his youthful experience in Sarawak and his mature administration of Perak was a long and lonely twenty-nine-year stretch on the moribund and fever-ridden island of Labuan, which had a population of some six thousand and an annual revenue of about £4,000. As the island's Colonial Secretary, Low painstakingly performed a series of thankless routine tasks in the hope of eventual preferment and, in his off-duty hours, made a number of intrepid botanical expeditions into the interior of neighbouring Borneo; he was the first known European to climb Mount Kinabalu and he published the first standard work on the *Inhabitants and Productions* of Sarawak.

When the well-merited preferment to the Perak Residency finally came, Low was fifty-three years old. His body was well toughened against the hazards and debilitations of tropical living and his mind was well disciplined by the long acceptance of isolation, disappointment and monotony. His beloved young wife had succumbed to Labuan's virulent fevers after only three years of marriage and his beloved only daughter, Kitty, had married John Pope-Hennessy, later the Governor of Hong Kong, and had left him to become the Governor's lady. Low disliked his pushy, brilliant son-in-law and the sentiment was more than reciprocated. In consequence he saw little of his daughter and so went to Perak with few personal commitments or professional expectations – other than that of proving his worth to his superiors at last. Certainly there was ample scope for initiative and individual decision-making: Low later reported that when he visited the Colonial Office before leaving for his post and, in the course of conversation, asked an official the name of the principal Raja he was being sent to "advise", the reply was "We don't know of one. You must try to ascertain whether there is anyone fit for the position and then he will be supported."

When he arrived, Low discovered that Raja Yusuf, the man whose earlier claims to the Perak throne had been passed over by the British, was now considered the most fit for the position of Perak's Chief Native Authority, so he settled at Kuala Kangsa, the small town where Yusuf lived. His Residency stood on a jungly hill overlooking a wide sweep of waters where the River Kangsa joined the River Perak, one hundred and fifty miles from the sea. A long flight of steps led from the riverside jetty to the Residency – an attap-thatch and wood bungalow of the kind which the local Chinese craftsmen could erect so cheaply and so well. At first it was, Low wrote, "miserably uncomfortable for want of furniture", for he had brought with him from Labuan only a few chairs, a portrait of James Brooke, and his large pigeon-holed desk, from which he began to administer the affairs of Perak.

The structural outline of administration was already in exist-ence. It consisted of an Assistant Resident, a Collector and Magistrate for the mining district of Larut, a Clerk of Court, an embryonic Customs Service, an Overseer of Rivers and Roads, a

Revenue Officer, a Shipmaster, a Surveyor, a Police Superintendent. But titles such as these were deceptive, for a man's department might consist of no more than a Eurasian clerk, a filing cabinet and a couple of guards housed in a thatched shed. Moreover, the calibre of appointees was not always high and this was to be expected for, at first, there were no fixed salary or pension schemes, rates of pay were low and the Peninsula was looked upon as a tropical white man's grave to which only the reckless or the desperate went. In a dispatch of 1879, Low complained angrily to the Colonial Office about "the useless loafers whom it was formerly the fashion to send on here, insolent, broken-down bankrupts or drunkards who all think themselves entitled to have and to express opinions contrary to the view of the Government".

Given the urgent need for reform in so many areas, Low felt that his top priority must be the improvement of the treasury and revenue services, for he was keenly aware of the financial realities – which were that the State itself had to afford to support a more efficient administration and become economically viable. This was the customary arrangement: the Residents and their Assistants were servants of the Crown under the authority of the Straits Settlements Government; they were appointed to the Malay States from the Colonial Service and were eligible for promotion to other colonies; but they were dependent on the States in which they resided for their salaries and, eventually, their pensions. Low's initial salary was £1,500 per annum and, Sir William Jervois pointed out to him, would remain so only "if the revenue of Perak is found sufficient to maintain the settlement at its present scale". Sir William's emphasis on stringency was in line with the British Government policy, which was extremely cautious about investing too much in the Malay States, while conscientious Residents like Hugh Low were equally concerned that the country should not be bled white by its foreign "advisers".

Obviously the solution was to increase the prosperity of Perak, which was loaded with debts when Low arrived. A main reason for this was that the Straits Settlements and the Colonial Office were still wrangling over the footing of the bill for that over-inflated Perak War. "Transport of Troops, Pay of Coolie Corps, Telegraph and Conveyance of Information, Furniture and Hospital Stores, Salaries of Officers, Military Auxiliary Arab Force" were among the items listed in an irate article in the *Straits Times* complaining that all this had nothing to do with them and should jolly well be paid for by Perak itself, which was presumed to be prospering mightily under the newly-established Pax Britannica. But in the late 1870s this was simply not the case.

Very few quality goods were produced, for only sultans and their retinues could afford to employ regularly craftsmen such as silversmiths, wood and metal workers. There was some trade in animal hides and horns, rattans and areca palms – the last a graceful slender-shafted tree which produced betel nuts, the stimulant that most Malays used as a substitute for the Koran-forbidden alcohol. A morsel of the nut was wrapped in a leaf of the betel, peppered with a little moistened lime and a brown, spicey paste; people chewing their betel quids looked as if their mouths were full of blood, which was rather disconcerting to European eyes. Other commodities of mainly local exchange were *gomuti* for the making of cordage used to capture alligators and tigers, and *jaggery*, a coarse sugar made from palm sap which was boiled to make a strong, very sweet liquor.

But the main source of revenue was still tin, even though many of the mines had remained unworked for several years, because of the disturbances of the Perak War. So Low travelled about talking tin prices with the Chinese mine-owners, and suggesting how they might get rid of the green veils of scum which floated atop the stagnant pits from which the coolies drew their drinking water, and how they might import portable centrifugal steam-pumps to replace the Chinese-style water-wheels which could neither prevent flooding of the mine-shafts during the wet season nor provide sufficient water during the dry.

A reliable water supply was essential because the tin ore was inconveniently mixed with detritus – pebbles, sand or stiff clay– which had to be sluiced away. In the early days disputes frequently arose because mines in favourable up-stream positions used up or diverted all the water from their down-stream competitors, until a ruling was made that every water-course should be in the absolute control of the State government and inspectors were appointed to see that it was obeyed. The proportion of ore found in the *kerang* or "wash-dirt" was usually quite high – after collecting samples from the Larut mines, Low reported that a coconut-shell full would yield up to an egg-cup full of tin. The once-washed material, the "tailings", were then re-sifted by those historically accustomed to making do with the left-overs: women, the elderly, and minority groups of labouring Indians or Siamese.

The layers of *kerang* were spread at irregular depths and had to be raised and stacked on the surface ready for sluicing. It was, as Frank Swettenham described it, a grim and arduous task: "The bottom of the mine is reached by step ladders made by cutting flat steps at an acute angle into the trunk of a tree. The Chinese run up and down these ladders with bare feet carrying baskets of soil slung at either end of a carrying stick ..." Under the fierce equatorial sun and the steaming rain; for up to ten hours a day, with nothing much at the end of it but a pot of tea, a bowl of rice, a scrap of dried fish, the occasional visit to the nearby gambling den or arrack shop, and a few puffs of opium to forget it all until dawn – when the weird wail of the wa-wa gibbon sounded from the jungle as the first light shone on the glossy banana leaves, and the water-wheels creaked into action again and the beat of a hollow gong summoned them from sleep. And the day began: cooked rice scooped from a coconut shell; the clearing of water that had collected in the workings during the night, the slinging of the baskets on to poles – then into the gritty depths, the nimble, leathery feet, soiled and sweaty, moving up and down the treacherous ladders, hour after weary hour.

When Hugh Low arrived, mining conditions were not much better than during the 1830s and 1840s when the first batches of unsuspecting coolies, mostly from South China, were persuaded with false promises to board Singapore-bound trading junks. At the end of horrific forty-day voyages they were sold – many of them unskilled and sickly – for a few dollars only, and sent to work in the mines of the Peninsula. The "advancers" or *towkay labur* – Chinese with sufficient capital to pay for the importation of the immigrants – were fairly ruthless, fairly rich and still in control of the mining scene when the British came.

Hard-headed though they were, Chinese mine-owners usually sought advice on the siting of any new enterprise from a Malay *pawang* – diviners who acted as mediators between the mines and the spirits of the tin. *Pawangs* alone were entitled to wear black coats near a mine or to eat food from any vessel not made of coconut-wood. They struck various postures to invoke the spirits of tin, which, they believed, was a volatile substance that could move around of its own accord. But their divining talents were not to be despised: the Chinese paid them handsomely for their help and Swettenham once wrote that "a Malay *pawang* has the same sort of nose for tin as a truffle dog has for truffles".

Once a mining site was determined upon, the *towkay laburs* put up a few rough sleeping sheds for the miners, with a nearby "death-shed" for the mortally sick, for miners did not like their comrades to die in the houses where they lived. The shed was usually a "lean-to hut with a roof just large enough to cover a mosquito-net", according to one observer. It was so small that, "during showers, the water splashes up from the ground and bespatters and saturates the sick man's couch and the mosquito-net around him drips with moisture whilst the chilly cold of early dawn makes his last moments replete with misery and discomfort".

For the still miserably living, the *towkays* put up notice boards stating the terms on which work was offered. Miners had their names put on the board which was a kind of contract whereby they contributed their labour in return for a mat in the sleeping-shed, basic food, work clothes, a little opium and the hope of a percentage share of any eventual profits. But ventures often failed and the profits from most of those that succeeded were creamed off by the mine-owners and the coolie brokers. The miners, forced into continual poverty and dependence, retaliated in the only way possible – by frequently absconding to other mines in search of better conditions.

Hugh Low soon realized that the system was, as he wrote, "a rotten one", and he tried to improve it by the standardization of labour contracts and the licensing of the coolie brokers, who recruited workers. He was also very concerned about the miners' miserable living conditions, both on humanitarian grounds and because he knew that the bulk of the State revenue depended, ultimately, on their labour. He tried to get rid of the dreadful death-sheds by opening the first hospital for miners in 1879, where the many who suffered from cholera, malaria or beri-beri could at least know the hope of cure.

But Low's greatest innovation during his early period of office was the State Council of Perak which, as Swettenham wrote, "acted as a safety valve for local discontents" and proved such a success that similar bodies were soon established in the other "Protected" States. Its function was to initiate regular consultation between the British and "influential natives and others", and the first Council was made up of Low, his assistant, William Maxwell, four Malay chiefs and two Capitans China (the term given to the leaders of each Chinese community).

The most important Malay councillor was Raja Yusuf, who seems to have been everybody's least favourite man. Miss Isabella Bird, who met him at Kuala Kangsa, soon after she left Douglas' Residency at Klang, described him as elderly, "with a grey moustache. His brow is a fine one and his face has a look of force, but the lower part of it is coarse and heavy." He had thrown in his lot with the British at the time of Birch's assassination and had been an enthusiastic supporter of their presence in the country ever since; he was, in fact, a collaborator and as such was unpopular among his own people and distrusted by the British. Swettenham thought him overbearing, rapacious, selfish and vindictive; Low, who had to cooperate closely with him, felt that his sole concept of government was that the peasants "were created to produce revenues for the Rajas and be at their entire disposal" and that Yusuf "cared for little but cases in which he has some hope of personal profit or satisfying personal spite". In a letter to the new Governor of the Straits Settlements, Sir William Robinson, Low said that Yusuf was "generally hated to

43

such an extent that he never could have suceeded if left to himself . . . and if I were only here to advise such a man and if he didn't believe I had authority to control his caprices when they are likely to be dangerous to the country, our hope of restoring peace to it would be vain and the position of Resident untenable."

In such circumstances, Low told Robinson, he had "to create the Government to be advised" and now that it was being created, he could not simply advise, he had to govern. Robinson, appreciating the inherent ambiguities of the Residential position, agreed that this was so, but cautioned, "All the same, the fiction (if such you prefer to call it) that the Residents are merely advisers must be kept up." And Sir Robert Meade of the Colonial Office, who joined in these crucial discussions about the Residents' functions, clarified but did not simplify the issue in an 1879 minute to the effect that "the better the Resident, the more power will be put into his hands by the people in their own interests, and so he must not be too good or he will become too powerful for a mere adviser"! By the following year Low had carried his point with his superiors and it was conceded that "in spite of the determination to assert officially that the Resident is only an adviser, he is in reality much more".

In Low's view, one of his major tasks was to protect the country from what he considered to be the excesses and failings of its own rulers – though, as has been later pointed out, the British were prone to brand the traditional obligations of kinship as nepotism and the customary perquisites of authority as bribery. To accustom the Malay rulers to Western ethical standards and to use their ambitions in unobtrusive furtherance of British policies, Low needed to gain their confidence and trust and he succeeded in this by keeping a sort of open house to which all might come and receive the benefits of his firm and patient paternalism.

"There have been rajas all day in the verandah and their followers sitting on the steps, all received by Mr Low with quiet courtesy and regaled with tea or coffee and cigarettes," Isabella Bird noted. Low's most constant visitor was Raja Yusuf, and "I humour him and I praise him where he deserves it", Low told the Colonial Office, describing his attempts to persuade the Raja to behave like a well-tamed British constitutional monarch, as a later historian has suggested. He urged Yusuf to conduct himself "like a raja instead of going into the bazaar and making himself so common" and to change his harsh and grasping ways so that he might become more generally popular. His efforts in the latter direction were not entirely successful; when Yusuf died ten years later his posthumous title was "the late Sultan, God pardon him".

In the meantime though the British needed Yusuf as a symbol of cooperative Malay sovereignty; Yusuf needed the British in order to retain his position at all; and the difficulties and potential flashpoints of the situation were contained within the institution of the State Council. Another good reason for the Council's existence was that it included Chinese headmen among its members. For until then the leaders of the two races had seldom sustained any constructive dialogue. The Malays had refused to acknowledge the political implications of the fact that the tin industry, which contributed most to the country's revenue, was Chinese-dominated at all levels; and the Chinese, for their part, had remained in self-sufficient communities and concentrated their efforts on economic expansion.

Such expansion flourished best in conditions of peace and order, so the Chinese generally welcomed the disciplines of the new British dispensation. In January 1878, when Governor Robinson visited the mining town of Taiping and was received by Resident Low and senior members of the Council, the local population, most of them Chinese, put on quite a show for him. The streets "had been decorated from end to end and at the expense of the inhabitants and of their own free will", Low noted in his journal. Firecrackers smoked, red banners flew, bands played, all "to convey the thanks of the Chinese community for English protection and their joy at His Excellency's intention to continue it". The scene "cannot but have been gratifying to His Excellency" Low added – and gratifying for Low too was such a demonstration of goodwill and seeming content in a State which less than three years before had supposedly been up in arms against the British.

Those most restive under the new order were the Malay chiefs who had been deprived of their customary sources of income when the Residents took over the collection and control of revenues. Writing of this, Low noted that Malays in general were unwilling "to adapt themselves to new circumstances and seek out unaccustomed means of subsistence" – and this was particularly true of the men in the various chiefs' entourages, many of whom became much impoverished and relied on the British to provide sufficient funds for them to maintain their former life-style.

This had been agreed in principle at Pangkor, but resources were insufficient to meet all their demands for money: "Everyone tugs at the unfortunate Resident for this same article," Low complained, when faced, for the third time, with the importunate mother-in-law of the exiled ex-Sultan Abdullah demanding financial support for her two nephews. However, he did what he could for her, in his unpretentious fashion, for "he speaks to Malays as respectfully as to Europeans", Isabella Bird noted, "neither lowering thereby his dignity nor theirs". And, "When a Malay with silent cat-like tread glides up the steps and appears on the verandah, Mr Low at once lays aside whatever he is doing and quietly gives himself to the business in hand."

The business varied in kind and importance: the theft of a couple of pigs perhaps, the trespass of a buffalo over a neighbour's paddy, a dispute between two fishermen about their fishing stakes in the Perak River; or, as details of the new rules and regulations filtered to the populace, there might be a deputation complaining about the proposed head tax on males over sixteen, or about the duties levied on the sale of firewood; Chinese came, to apply for a licence to open a new pawn shop or the monopoly right to cut attap leaves and shoots along a certain stretch of river-bank in order to make thatch for export; and sometimes people simply came to bring something quaint and curious for the Resident to see – a counting stick used by the aborigines, a rare species of whistling thrush. This informal, personal coming and going was very different from the martial rigidity of the Selangor Residency, as Isabella Bird pointed out, and it could only work in conditions of mutual trust – as Low demonstrated soon after his arrival, when he reduced the size of his police-force and appointed the *penghulus* (Malay village headmen) to be responsible for keeping the peace in their districts.

Such caring and conscientious endeavour took all Low's time and energy: "He works fourteen hours out of the twenty-four," Isabella Bird wrote. "I think that work is his passion and a change of work his sole recreation." He did have one other in fact – in the shapes of two tame apes, a large lively one, four foot high, called Mahmoud, of sombre and hairy visage, and one under two foot, with baby-like hands and a wistful expression, called Eblis, who was everyone's favourite. They were Low's comic, affectionate and constant companions, and Isabella Bird's description of their customary inclusion in the Kuala Kangsa dining arrangements is a collectors' item among the many bizarreries of the white man's behaviour on the Eastern scene.

In the dining-room the table was laid in the grand fashion, "with exquisite linen, china, crystal and flowers". A Sikh guard stood massively to attention in the doorway; a butler and a Malay lad served the food; a Chinese on the verandah steps swished a punkah. Miss Bird, who first arrived at the Residency in Low's absence, was shown to the table and Mahmoud and Eblis were led in by servants and sat down on their appropriate dining-chairs; Low's other pet, a retriever, was tied to Isabella's chair. "This was all done with the most profound solemnity. The circle being then completed, dinner proceeded with great stateliness. The apes had their curry, chutney, pineapples and bananas on porcelain plates and so had I. The chief difference was that whereas I waited to be helped, the big ape was impolite enough occasionally to snatch something from a dish as the butler passed round the table, and that the small one before very long migrated from his chair to the table and, sitting by my plate, helped himself daintily from it. What a grotesque dinner party! What a delightful one! My 'next of kin' were so reasonably silent; they required no conversational efforts; they were most interesting companions."

The two creatures followed Low wherever he went, looking, says Miss Bird, "exactly like familiar demons and certainly anyone having them about him two hundred years ago would have been burned as a wizard". Low was equally devoted to his pets – though Mahmoud could be rather trying on occasions, as on the day that he soaked his fingers in an inkpot on the desk and rubbed them thoroughly over the clean and careful dispatch that Low had just written to the Secretary of State in London. Low, following the legendary forbearance of Isaac Newton on a similar occasion, apparently took Mahmoud in his arms and said, "Poor creature, you've given me a great deal of trouble but you know no better."

Ignorance could not excuse Mahmoud for his bullying of Eblis, however, whom he used sometimes to beat harshly with a malacca cane. Mahmoud also had the unamiable trait of throwing bananas or cushions very accurately at people who irritated him, and he was inordinately fond of champagne, which Low served when he had special guests for tiffin. On one such occasion, Isabella Bird recorded, the ape quaffed a very large glass, after which "he tried to seem sober and sit up but could not, then staggered to a chair, trying hard to walk steadily and nodding his head with a would-be witty but really obfuscated look, then finding he could not sit up, he reached a cushion and lay down, very nearly resting his head on his elbow and trying to look reasonable, but not succeeding and then he fell asleep . . ."

Tiny, bewitching Eblis was less boisterous, more affectionate and used to sit for hours on Low's shoulder with his arms round his neck and murmuring "ouf, ouf" in the manner of his kind. When the little creature fell ill, Low nursed him like a baby, feeding him milk and morsels of banana at regular intervals. It was indicative of the man's emotional solitude that, when writing to his daughter Kitty of the situation, he told her that, except for herself, he "cared for Eblis more than anything in the world".

Apart from the antics of Mahmoud and the sudden unpredictable and riotous descent of a partially-tamed siamang (gibbon) who dwelled among the roof-rafters, the Kuala Kangsa Residency was a haven of quiet orderliness. "It is hot, silent, tropical," wrote

The Pangkor Engagement of 1874: 4. Sir Andrew Clarke, 5. James Birch, 5a. Frederick McNair, 6. Tristram Speedy, 7. Frank Swettenham

Chinese houses and a Malay bathing-shed on the River Kangsa

Swettenham and Speedy in Kuala Kangsa during the military
occupation after Birch's murder

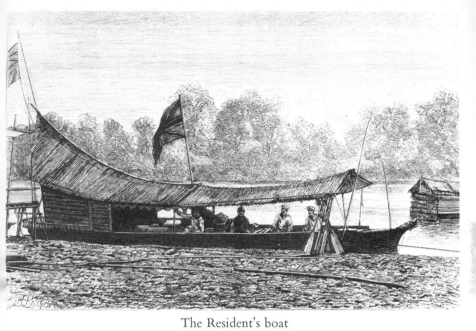

The Resident's boat

A Malay dug-out on the River Perak

James and Emily Innes' bungalow at Langat

A street in Kuala Kangsa

Isabella Bird travelling through Perak

Hugh Low, with Raja Yusuf seated in the centre and his son-in-law,
Raja Idris, on his right

Kuala Lumpur: its early days in 1882

The Government Offices later built in Kuala Lumpur

The Residency in Kuala Lumpur of 1882

The later Residency of 1896

Yap Ah Loy, Capitan
China of Kuala Lumpur

William Maxwell

Hugh Low

Frederick Weld

Taiping seen from the Residency on Maxwell Hill, 1882

A street in Taiping, *c.* 1890

Tin-mining in Larut, *c.* 1890

Railway construction

Hugh Clifford and
Martin Lister in 1886

Hugh Clifford

Clifford's house in Pahang, 1896

Henry Ridley

Leonard Wray

Richard Winstedt

Frank Swettenham

The Conference of 1903: Swettenham, in the centre, is flanked by the four Sultans, on his right Perak (Raja Idris) and Selangor, on his left Negri Sembilan and Pahang

Miss Bird one afternoon during her stay. "The sound of Mr Low's busy pen alone breaks the stillness during much of the day; so silent is it that the first heavy drops of the daily tropical shower on the roof have a startling effect." After the shower, as breeze-bringing twilight approached, new sounds began: the insects of the night tuned up; from the village below came the sweet hum of wind-bells hung in the trees; people splashed and bathed in the cool lemon-light river; paddles knocked against the sides of some slim, slow-moving boat; the Residency elephant trumpeted for his evening meal; night-jars began their "chunk-king"; green pigeons with bright orange breasts, who had been searching for berries in the forest, squawked as they came home to roost among the mangrove swamps; and, as dark deepened, there sometimes came the sound of the *pungyok*, a small brown owl with a plaintive voice said by the Malays to be the moon's lover.

At such an hour, Hugh Low at last laid down his busy pen and went for a stroll with the apes and the dog round the Residency garden, where he was beginning to experiment with the growing of a variety of tropical crops, and the keeping of goats and Nellore cows imported from India. After the customary stately and silent dinner with his two companions, he retired early to his bed-mat, his rest occasionally disturbed by the roar of a tiger, the crash of some rogue elephant trying to break into a banana plantation nearby, the drum and pipe of a late-night festival celebrating the marriage of a village maiden with henna-dyed hands and feet.

It was a tough and lonely life, but satisfying for a man of his temperament, experience and ability. During 1879 – the year that Isabella Bird visited him at Kuala Kangsa – Low permitted himself some cautious acknowledgment of his own success. He wrote to the Colonial Office in July that "the peace of the country is now thoroughly established and all the population have a thorough confidence in the Government to an extent which I didn't venture to expect could possibly be brought about in so few years". And indeed, whatever the Colonial Office's miscalculations of past appointees, it was evident that this time they had picked a winner, for there can have been few men to have pursued a career of comparably demanding responsibility in the Service for a decade and to have had so few criticisms levelled against them. As a later historian describes it, "In so far as there was any system at all about the work of the British Resident in the early years of this experiment, it was Hugh Low who created it."

5

"Virtually a dictator"

During the early years of Low's administration at Kuala Kangsa, his Assistant Resident was William Edward Maxwell, a man in his early thirties, severe-looking, of medium height, with a yellow moustache and piercing eyes. Isabella Bird described him as being "able, combative, dogmatic, well-read and well-informed, expresses himself incisively, is self-reliant, strong-willed, thoroughly just, thoroughly a gentleman and has immense energy and business capacity ... talks well, but with much perfectly good-natured vehemence ..." In a private letter she added that he was also "bumptious and without tenderness".

Part of the reason for Maxwell's knowledgeable and rather imperious self-assurance, upon which others also commented adversely, was that he sprang from one of the relatively few English families who, at that time, had accumulated fairly long experience of the area. His father was Sir Peter Benson Maxwell who had written so critically about the conduct of the Perak War in a cogent and contentious pamphlet called *Our Malay Conquests*. Its main drift was that the British intervention in the internal affairs of the native Malay States had been totally without justification and that the Pangkor Engagement was a treacherous piece of diplomatic trickery and international politicking. It was, he pointed out, "binding only on the weaker of the two parties", that is, the Malays who, "while they imagine they were treating for a guide, had accepted a master and signed away their country to foreign rule".

Sir Peter's brand of outspoken, unillusioned liberalism and his sense of responsibility and sympathy for Malays influenced his sons, three of whom followed so closely in his footsteps that they all held junior posts in the Straits Settlements Court Offices in 1865 when their father was Recorder of Penang. William, the second son, was educated at Repton, went out to Singapore when he was nineteen, quickly learned fluent Malay, qualified as an advocate at the local Bar in 1867, and, during the next eight years, held a variety of magisterial posts in the Peninsula, where he gained considerable understanding of and liking for the country. His brusque manner and indefatigable appetite for information and hard work did not make him very popular with his colleagues and the general verdict was: one of Frank Swettenham's ilk, rather too big for his youthful boots.

During the Perak War Maxwell was made a deputy commissioner for the Larut Field Force which, in Low's view, was something of a disadvantage when he later became Assistant Resident. Commenting on Maxwell in his journal, Low wrote, "He is a splendid fellow . . . but he is a little rough and hasty in his ways with the natives, especially the inferior classes, and the part he took in the War is, I expect, against him with the Perak Malays for the present." The Malays in question nicknamed Maxwell "The Tiger Cub" and "The Cat-Eyed One" because he had the habit of jerking his eyeglass into position and thus concentrating a penetratingly watchful glare from his light blue eyes which frequently made the weaker quail.

However, Maxwell's respect for Malay culture was genuine and he was determined to frame laws that would promote order and efficiency in the country and, at the same time, exist in harmony with native custom. However, his European training had imbued him with the concept of law as a fixed code which could ideally be applied in accordance with precedent and without fear or favour under all circumstances. Such crystallization of justice into an abstract and universal ideal was quite alien to Malay thought; in their experience the dispensing of rewards and punishments was arbitrary and flexible, dependent entirely on the relative power of the various chiefs, their networks of clan loyalty and their concern to maintain overall social cohesion in a given place at any particular time. It was an approach which Low and

Maxwell used to illustrate by citing the case of a man charged with murder who was brought before a jury of local worthies. They all found him guilty – except for one chief who, when asked how he could disregard such damning evidence against the accused, replied, "What do I care for evidence? This man is my follower."

One of Maxwell's first tasks in Perak was the drawing up of regulations concerning land tenure. This was not easy, for he soon found that land ownership was based on unwritten laws of inheritance and occupation. "It was the custom," wrote Swettenham of this period, "for anyone to settle where he pleased on unoccupied and unclaimed land and leave it when he felt inclined." Cultivators of this kind had no legal title to any of the land, "but chiefs of districts and others with official positions – some indeed without – possessed written documents investing them with extraordinary powers over large and ill-defined areas."

The very idea therefore of land as a marketable commodity was alien to the country; nevertheless, Maxwell's terms of reference were definite and in 1879 he produced a code of land regulations for Perak which divided the State's land into four categories: that occupied by natives under Malay tenure; building land in towns and villages; mining reserves; and what he rather misleadingly termed "waste land" which was available for agricultural purposes. Embodied in the regulations were the concepts of, on the one hand, allowing considerable latitude for the development of agriculture by foreign investors, and, on the other, the preservation of as much as possible of the native rural identity. They were designed, one historian has suggested, "to prevent the inroads of Chinese immigration into the Malay countryside – that idyllic Malay *kampong* which sustained the preeminent position of the Resident as legal guardian, intercessor and protector". As such they found favour with the Government and the 1879 Perak Regulations were adopted in the other Native States in due course.

As the Resident's law and order man, Maxwell was also concerned with the framing of new legislation and improving the existing judiciary system. He worked out the first regulations enforcing the isolation of villages at times of cholera or beri-beri outbreak and others defining specific areas of responsibility for the various Government officials. Then there were the monthly financial estimates to work out – for supplying the Perak police-stations with oil-lamps, the prisoners with rations and blankets, the policemen with clothing and breech-load rifles sent from England. The State's Annual Report of 1878 drew attention to the need for new and improved prisons, for, in some districts, prisoners were "confined in cages built in or under the police-station, sleeping for the most part on planks placed upon the ground". It was supposed that they frequently contracted beri-beri because of the "cold winds which nightly descend from the mountains" and certainly they were prone to cholera because they were given "a most noxious slimy-greenish fluid to drink".

The plan was to get the prisoners out of their cages and doing some useful work – as breakers of granite, sawyers of wood, makers of roads. The last was a top priority, for the so-called roads that connected the mines and villages with the riverine shipping places were in a shocking state, pitted with holes so deep that "cartloads of large stones were no sooner thrown into them than they disappeared into the bog beneath as the next cart passed over them". But the administration did not want to be over-burdened with convict labour, which was expensive to support in any even half-humanitarian fashion, and also a potential source of unrest. So it was to help cut down the prison population that first Low and then the other Residents decided to make the *penghulus* responsible for local law and order and the punishment of petty crime.

Penghulus were the traditional authority figures on the Malay scene – the village headmen who acted as links between the villagers and the district chiefs. Under the new regime, *penghulus* were selected and supervised by the Residents, from whom they received their insignia of office. Under the new regime too the duties of a *penghulu* – which Maxwell helped to define – multiplied exceedingly. They became the official chroniclers of births and deaths; the disseminators of government instructions; the labour contractors for the proliferation of small-scale public works; the collectors of land-rents, the dispensers of licences for fishing stakes, timber-cutting, the collection of gutta percha. The perks of the position included a pension, a house-site and garden free of land-rent and the halo of official, if circumscribed, authority. But a good *penghulu* had to be a diligent and honest man and the accounts of *penghulu* conduct that were forwarded to Hugh Low by his field staff varied from the highly satisfied to the totally despairing.

William Maxwell's instinct was to uphold and increase the authority of the *penghulu* because it was an hereditary and traditionally Malay post, and Maxwell was a "Malay man" who disliked and distrusted the Chinese. Such bias in favour of one race or the other was commonplace and most of the early administrators were Malay men, partly, undoubtedly, because they mixed less with the Chinese and few understood their language. Also, the Chinese were often labelled as being "unruly", "impudent" and rather too good at making money for the British liking. "They are the bees that suck the honey from every profitable undertaking," wrote Frank Swettenham disdainfully. And again, "It is almost hopeless to expect to make friends with a Chinaman ... The Chinese, at least that class of them met with in Malaya, do not understand being treated as equals; they realize only two positions – the giving and the receiving of orders." Malays, by contrast, seemed to approximate much more comfortably to the concept of the noble, innocently indolent and tractable "native" whom the British had come to "protect".

But the Chinese had their supporters, especially among those who admired their enterprising get-up-and-go – a valuable attribute for colonizers and immigrants alike. William Hornaday, the American naturalist, passing through a rural district near Kuala Lumpur, noted that "there were houses and huts of both Malays and Chinese scattered along the road and the two could always be distinguished at a glance. Those of the Chinese were always in good repair and surrounded by flourishing and beautifully kept vegetable gardens of one or two acres. The houses of the Malays were always in bad repair and their gardens, when they had any, were neglected and weedy. Every Chinese we met or saw was carrying something, or else at work in his garden. Every Malay was either strolling along empty-handed or else loafing in the door of his hut. If Singapore were my territory, I would give it to the Chinese."

Considering Maxwell's predisposition towards the Malays, it was perhaps unfortunate that he spent much of his time as Low's Assistant in the Residency at Taiping, capital of the Chinese-dominated province of Larut, where, according to Isabella Bird who visited him there, he "ruled rigidly", and was "virtually a dictator". Much of his power was magisterial and he spent many hours exercising it in the crowded court-room where most of the offenders were Chinese commonly accused of such crimes as petty larceny, drunkenness, assault, and the abduction of women.

There was always a shortage of women among the Chinese population and those who were there frequently led fraught and miserable lives, as suggested by the pathetic shred of personal history recounted by one Si Ah Kam in Maxwell's court: "I was kidnapped from China eight years ago and brought to Penang by Ly Ah Sam who sold me to the Si Yip and they took me to Tai Kong where I was a prostitute. Uh Ah Fat redeemed me and when the disturbances in the mines broke out, my husband and I ran away, but the Si Yip took us prisoners and after robbing us, they allowed my husband to go but they sold me to the Goh Guan Kongese, they paying twenty-five dollars for me. I was taken away by one Sam See. I wish to go to Penang to Uh Ah Fat, my former husband . . ." As Maxwell could not understand these sad case-histories at first hand, he had to rely on interpreters. It was not a satisfactory arrangement, for there was no guarantee that the interpreters were trustworthy or competent. When Maxwell graded them on their translating abilities he labelled most "middling to poor", and one Oh Koon Choon he also described as being "hard of hearing, stubborn, proud and a great bore to the sitting magistrate".

Maxwell's seat of power was the large, lofty Residency built by Captain Speedy, but, since the departure of that big spender, it was run on much more frugal and workmanlike lines. "There are no ornaments or superfluities," reported Isabella Bird. "There are two simple meals daily, with tea and bananas at seven a.m. and afternoon tea at five p.m.", and that was all, for "Mr Maxwell is most abstemious". The main attraction of Maxwell's table was the conversation round it, and Miss Bird's description of a dinner party she shared there with Major Paul Swinburne and Maxwell relieves the usually rather dour picture of the latter. Swinburne was a cousin of the poet, Algernon, and had a reputation for brilliant invective delivered in a cool aristocratic style: "Mr Maxwell fought for victory and Major Swinburne to beat him and the row was deafening ... An energetic difference seems of daily occurrence and possibly is an essential ingredient of friendship ... Major Swinburne, in an aggravating tone, begins with some peculiarity or foible, real or supposed, of his friend. With a deluge of sarcasm, mimicry and ridicule torments him mercilessly, and, without giving him time to reply, disappears, saying Parthian-like, 'Now my dear fellow, it's no use resenting it, you haven't such another friend as me in the world – you know if it were not for me, you'd be absolutely intolerable' ...." And this was just the way to deal with Maxwell who enjoyed a really fierce argument above all things – though he was inclined to ride roughshod over his opponents if he could. As one of his critics described it, "Any committee on which he served tended either to become a one-man show or end in deadlock."

However protracted the disputations of the night before, Maxwell was at his desk by eight o'clock each morning where he received a constant stream of visitors in an "air of business without fuss", as Miss Bird says. Occasionally, beset by a particularly knotty problem over a boundary dispute or the levying of tin revenue, he would stroll along the huge verandah which reminded Miss Bird of "the fore-cabin of a great Clyde steamer" and from which, captain-fashion, he could survey the scene below. In the distance, neat Chinese villages cut out of the jungle and the hillocks of exhausted tin-workings; nearer at hand, the white-painted bungalows where his staff lived, a hospital and a row of shops to supply the needs of the miners who came crowding in from the mines on their off-duty hours filling the gambling and opium dens, the brothels and the clan-meeting halls.

More certain now of their small pleasures, their meagre rewards, the miners were much more orderly and peaceful than a few years before and the Residency's strong force of Sikhs and Pathans helped to keep them that way. The force was under the command of Major Swinburne, who kept it in good martial trim. It was made up of "splendid-looking men", Miss Bird thought; they wore blue turbans, scarlet coats and white trousers, and sported "long moustaches and whiskers ... sober, docile and peaceful", though, according to their commander, inclined to "indulge in violent wordy warfare on theological subjects". Their methods of peace-keeping were somewhat summary: "One sees a single Sikh driving four or five Chinamen in front of him having knotted their pigtails together for reins," Miss Bird noted.

Maxwell's other occupation, when he was not working or arguing, was the study of Malayan literature and folk-lore, for he was generally acknowledged to be the most erudite among his generation of "scholarly administrators". He was an early expert on the lore of the village *pawangs* (the diviners and medicine men) and on the pithy Malay proverbs, which he published in rather turgid detail for the Straits Settlements branch of the Royal Asiatic Society, of which he was a founder member. Lest such pursuits seemed too frivolous, Maxwell used to preface his translations by explaining that "the stock-in-trade of these rural *savants* ... gives one insight into their modes of thought and their motives of action, and from the principles inculcated it is possible to form some estimate of the vices they condemn and the virtues they admire".

Maxwell delighted in discovering the similarities between the wise saws of English countryfolk and those which the Malay peasantry expressed in terms of their own rural experience: "though you may feed a jungle fowl off a gold plate, it will return to the jungle again nevertheless" was the Malay equivalent of the silk purse and the sow's ear, and the Malay version of the frying-pan into the fire was "from the jaws of a crocodile to the mouth of a tiger". The field of study was rich, for every Malayan river, forest and village was mantled with legends and stories of goblins and spirits, whose strange antics the locals discussed in an intimate

58

and matter-of-fact fashion, "like a housewife might talk of ants in the kitchen", as one official put it. Some spirits were prone to take up temporary abode in the bodies of albino buffaloes, tigers, pigs, cats or elderly women; others, more benevolent, used to go singing down the rivers in phantom boats late at night and plant magic rice in the paddies for the villagers.

The intense interest which Maxwell developed in the culture of the country and his proven capacity for painstaking and diligent work made him a generally satisfactory Assistant in the eyes of his superior, Hugh Low. Though Low, like most people, respected rather than liked him, for, he noted, Maxwell also had "several objectionable little habits" which would soon be cured "by my occasionally drawing attention to them" – which Low, twenty years the senior, did not fail to do. But Frank Swettenham, who was of the same generation and of a similarly ambitious, industrious and autocratic temperament, did not get on with Maxwell at all.

The two men soon began to differ vehemently in their views on the conduct of Malay administration. Maxwell, who was a firm believer in hierarchical discipline, believed that the Residents and their Assistants should be subject to strong directives and supervision from the Straits Settlements Government and the Colonial Office. Swettenham, whose instincts were, at this time, more expansionist and *laissez-faire*, urged that, if the Residents were allowed greater freedom of action, they would be the better able to steer each State on its separate and flexible course. As long as Swettenham and Maxwell were both in relatively subordinate positions where their policy-making powers were limited, these differences simmered under the surface, but later their disagreements sharpened and they each sought allies among the officials of the Colonial Office – many of whom were more familiar than their ministers with Malayan affairs and held strong views of their own about how these should be conducted. They were, too, well aware of the clash of personality involved: ". . . Neither of these men can give an unbiased opinion about the other," ran one Colonial Office minute on the subject of Swettenham and Maxwell's acrimonious relationship, ". . . which is a great pity for they are two very able fellows." By 1880 those abilities and their unusual grasp and experience of Malay affairs had marked them both out for promotion – and for rivalry. And, in the next decade, their mutual dislike congealed into a strong antipathy which was to have its effect on the country's political development.

6

"A number of thatched hovels"

At some unspecified date during 1860 or 1861 a few poor Chinese traders belonging to the Hokkein clan paddled up the Klang River to where it joined the River Gomback, the furthest navigable point to which boats could carry supplies intended for the tin-mines at nearby Ampang. The confluence of the waterways seemed a good place to set up shop, which the Chinese successfully did. As the mines flourished, more miners arrived with a little more money to spend and in due course a rough-and-ready trading settlement grew up in the jungle clearing, inhabited mostly by Chinese.

The Malay chiefs indigenous to the area had control of the tin revenues, but squabbled over them constantly and each raja who could rustle up sufficient supplies of gunpowder, muskets and followers to fire them held the rich upper hand until he was overthrown by some neighbouring rival. As more Chinese immigrants arrived they too divided into factions and went storming into combat with daggers and swords, wooden shields, protective dried skins bound across their chests and helmets made of coconut shells.

A man called Ah Sze of the Hokka clan, an early arrival on the scene, never joined in these frays for he was of a mild disposition (and was called "Sweet Potato Ah Sze" in consequence). Wisely, he devoted his energies to trade instead and was soon one of the wealthiest men along the Klang River. Ah Sze had a friend of a more combative and ambitious disposition who was manager of a successful tin-mine at Ampang. His name was Yap Ah Loy, a peasant's son who had been shipped to Malaya in

1854 when he was seventeen and full of hope, though his property consisted of no more than "eighty dollars in Chinese currency and a few cheap pieces of luggage", according to his biographer. For Yap Ah Loy eventually rated a biography – as the dynamic creator of a place called Kuala Lumpur.

Energetic and versatile like most of the self-made, Yap Ah Loy had been a miner, a cook, a pig-dealer and a "head fighter" before, in 1865, he opened Kuala Lumpur's first drugstore. The following year, Ah Sze was offered the position of Capitan China for the growing township but, true to his nickname, he declined such a tough and competitive assignment and nominated his friend instead. Yap Ah Loy accepted with alacrity and was ceremonially acknowledged Capitan by the Malays, for which occasion he wore the costume and head-dress of a raja.

In the early years of Yap Ah Loy's reign the inconclusive internecine warfare continued. Frank Swettenham, one of the very few Englishmen to visit it at that period, wrote that "the normal state" of the area was "robbery, battle and murder", and that Kuala Lumpur itself consisted of a "number of thatched hovels" dotted haphazardly on the jungle fringes. Swettenham went into one hovel which appeared empty and was so – "except for a dead Chinaman with a bullet hole in his chest who was sitting on the red earth floor with his back against the wall". Yap Ah Loy proved friendly and invited Swettenham and his companion to stay at his home. To provide them with knives and forks, he graciously melted down a number of Mexican dollars, which "was very thoughtful", Swettenham noted, "but the forks, being of pure silver, bent under the slightest pressure and had to be constantly straightened in order to carry food". All in all, the settlement was just too isolated to be of much potential, Swettenham felt: from it, "a few miles of rough unmetalled cart-track ran north and south to other smaller mining camps. For the rest, there was unbroken forest and a very sparse population."

As the British were not over-anxious to move into such unpromising interiors, Kuala Lumpur remained, for most of the 1870s, little more than a trading and shanty town, three days' boat journey upstream from Klang. A couple of muddy streets led from the landing stage to the open market, a gambling shed roofed with jungle rollers, a few provision shops, opium dens, brothels, workshops for the repair of mine-machinery. In the even muddier undrained alleys behind was a jumble of pig sties and slaughter houses so that Kuala Lumpur was early renowned for its stinks.

Yap Ah Loy, the born entrepreneur, never afraid of taking a full-scale Chinese risk, teetering often on the verge of bank-ruptcy, was owner of the grandest house in town. Taking his whack from the profits of the gambling and opium enterprises he owned, he nevertheless ploughed some of the money back into a primitive hospital for the miners, a school and various new ventures such as a tapioca farm, a sugarcane plantation, a brick-making factory and the first steam-pump to be used in the mines. By 1879 there were about two thousand people living in the area, most of them Chinese males who frequently shifted about in search of better working conditions or the promise of a full-scale tin bonanza. That year there was a definite boom in tin prices, more people were attracted to the Ampang mines and the British belatedly realized the strategic importance of moving further into the Selangor interiors.

The realization did not please Captain Bloomfield Douglas who, late in 1879, was ordered to uproot his frail and timid entourage from dreary Klang to this even more isolated and ramshackle settlement. Typically, he decided to site his new Residency on the opposite bank away from the clang and stink of the central town; scary as ever, his first priority was to get a barracks built for his police-force, with a cleared square where they could parade in showy strength. And he appointed his son-in-law, Dominic Daly, as the first permanent official – which proved to be another of his many Malayan mistakes.

Yap Ah Loy did not particularly warm to this British move either, for he guessed that it signalled the eventual end of his hegemony; he also believed however that, though he had a great hold over the Chinese community, the best chance of lasting economic and social stability would be under a British administra-tion – which, in turn, recognized his authority as Capitan China and appointed him to the first Selangor State Council. So, in 1880, when the new Governor of the Straits Settlements, Sir Frederick Weld, paid his first visit to the new capital, all was sweetness and light. There was feasting and speeches and, in the little wooden theatre, Weld was treated to a performance put on by actors dressed in scarlet, blue and gold silks depicting all the rival factions "giving up their quarrels and putting themselves under the Governor's protection and doing him homage". Weld, formerly a Governor of Western Australia and Tasmania, always felt he had a special mission to "civilize the natives" and, according to the modern historian Emily Sadka, "lived in a perpetual cloud of sentiment and patriarchial goodwill towards the peoples in his charge". He took an immense interest, therefore, in the affairs of the Malay States and was surprised and delighted by the display of so much dutiful loyalty in these Selangor backwoods. On his return to Singapore, he wrote to his superiors prophesying exciting and prosperous times ahead for Kuala Lumpur.

His prediction was correct, but the good times could not begin as long as the administration was in the hands of Bloomfield Douglas, for whom the raw disorder of the place soon proved altogether too much. He came into conflict with Yap Ah Loy, who was not impressed by his bluster and bombast; moreover, his credibility with the Straits Settlements Government was wearing very thin: "His Excellency directs that Mr Daly should at once survey and report upon the land claims of the Capitan China with a view to fixing their position and extent and finally settling the question in a fair spirit," was one of the many stern directives Douglas received at the time when Yap Ah Loy was seeking to secure leases of valuable land in the township's growing centre. Douglas pleaded for more time, for help with the trigonometrical surveys; the reports he eventually submitted were severely criticized for a "lack of statistical detail and figures to support statements".

Nor was the Secretariat satisfied with the progress of the road-building programme. "What did all these coolies *do* on this stretch of road?" asked an official suspiciously, after receiving a large bill of costs. "If you can't find out, visit the place and send a report. Where does this road go to and from? How long is it now? Is it a cart-road or what?" Lacking trust in Douglas' judgment, the inquisitive officials in Singapore did not help matters by sending him a string of commands and countermands about licences, import duties, pension allowances, and Douglas made matters worse by trying to push through some absurd regulations of his own – as, for example, that all washermen should be licensed.

Soon Frank Swettenham was round on one of his busy investigatory tours and he reported back to headquarters that the State Council which Douglas had started was not nearly so effective as Hugh Low's because he had not won the confidence of the native chiefs and headmen. Swettenham also found that Douglas' revenue estimates were faulty, his judicial administration inadequate and his allocation of funds injudicious; most serious of all, the affairs of the Land Office were not only hopelessly muddled but highly suspect. The suspicion was that Douglas, his son-in-law and other public officers on the staff had been engaged in speculative land deals from which they had made considerable profit.

When Sir Frederick Weld heard about all this, he was in a quandary. He felt sure that the charges were at least partly true, but could they be made to stick – and if they did he would have a full-blown scandal on his hands which certainly would not enhance the image of British administration in the eyes of the natives. Then James Innes who, with poor Emily, had been consigned to yet another dismal riverine swamp, entered the lists, accusing Douglas of various corrupt practices over the years – in particular of making profits from the Sultan of Selangor's official allowance. This he had done, Innes claimed, by deducting money from it for such dubious supplies as "a horse and carriage, portraits of Queen Victoria and Prince Albert, guns, wines, an old broken piano, English crockery and cutlery etc". Innes added that the old Sultan had protested these extravagances, saying that he had never fired an English gun in his life, that he preferred walking to driving in a carriage, that he ate with his fingers, not with English forks, that the Koran forbade drinking spirits and that he could not play the piano. (Apparently he liked the pictures.)

Douglas denied some of the charges, but justified a portion of the expenditure on the grounds that, whether the Sultan liked it or not, it was proper for him to be equipped with "those things natives of the higher classes now provide for the entertainment of European visitors ... Has the Sultan," he inquired of the Colonial Office, "to remain in the same barbarous state I found him in 1875?" Weld disliked and distrusted Innes' shrill accusations as much as Douglas' blustering deviousness and, early in 1882, he decided to go again to Kuala Lumpur to see for himself what was happening.

He discovered that things really were in a mess. Dwellings and offices had been built of highly inflammable and flimsy materials and were liable to flooding at every monsoon – except for the brick-built Residency on the hill; the hospital – adapted from a former bullock-shed – had a leaking roof and noisome latrines; and the town's sanitation in general was appalling because all the road drains had been badly made and kept blocking up. Morale among Douglas' staff was low: there had undoubtedly been some fiddling of the accounts; the chief surgeon of the hospital was usually drunk; officers of the Public Works Department did not turn up for work until eleven o'clock, so the clerks did not bother to arrive until fifteen minutes before.

Following this second investigation, Douglas was forced to resign quietly from the Service in August 1882, though Weld was reluctant to treat him too harshly, on the grounds that, in spite of his failings, he was "courageous, energetic and zealous in many directions". He also pleaded with the Colonial Office to grant Douglas some pension, because "... he is an old man and cannot work much longer. He has an old and feeble wife and a nearly dumb daughter afflicted with mental incapacity; a boy too, now at school. Absolute ruin for them is a heavy punishment for anything less than actual corruption." The Colonial Office duly decided that "absolute corruption" had not occurred and that Douglas' faults were "general slackness and nepotism rather than downright dishonesty". They paid him a temporary allowance and his fare home – from where Douglas managed to bluff his way into the Canadian Marine and Fisheries Department and went off to Ottawa.

Douglas' departure was an ill wind that blew somebody some good, or, as the Malays put it, "When the junk sinks, the shark has its fill". In December 1882, Frank Swettenham, just thirty-two years old, was appointed the new Resident of Selangor. For Weld, it was "such a relief" to have him in the post instead of Douglas; for Swettenham, it was the post he had coveted for several years and, anyway, as he wrote in his later reminiscences, no one else was as well qualified: "When I went to Selangor in 1882 I knew the country from end to end and all influential Malays from the Sultan downwards. The State was very thinly peopled, especially as regards Malays. They were scattered about in squalid villages, neglected plantations and groups of a few huts whose inhabitants eked out a miserable existence by cultivating an acre of rice and a few fruit trees or by fishing."

So much hopeless "backwardness" was obviously ripe for the ministrations of a new broom like Swettenham who enthusiastically set about banishing the evils of "misery", "squalor" and "neglect" from the land. The estimates of expenditure he submitted for the first year of his office suggest the range of his proposed activities in this cause: "To Education and Medical, salaries of Collectors, police, gaols, marine expenses, launches etc., conveyance of mails, transport, field allowances for officers and surveyors and miscellaneous prospecting. Steward at the Rest House, re-siting of the Pauper Hospital near the swamp. Expense of clearing the river, constructing a new jetty, purchasing of survey instruments, the construction of brick drains to replace the useless ones in the Kuala Lumpur streets . . ."

A very urgent task, Swettenham went on to say, was the building of a "system of roads where none existed", and certainly he was right, to judge by the account of a traveller heading for Kuala Lumpur in 1883 who walked for days along jungle tracks between the occasional, isolated villages. Each house, he wrote, "had a rough shelter for passers-by in which hung sundry branches of shrivelled plantains for sale and which were occupied by half-naked children who made these sheds their playground. Here the traveller rested awhile before attempting to cross the swamp, full of rank grasses and rushes and waist-deep in mud, that stretched across his path."

So Swettenham sent forth surveyors accompanied by two coolies apiece to carry their instruments, a canteen of cooking pots, a bed-roll and a rush mat. As one of the surveyor's reports suggests, however, such terrain was not going to be easily subdued by quadrant and macadam: "You will see," he explained to Swettenham, who had been making impatient enquiries as to what he had been doing out there in the jungle for so long, ". . . that a great many days were spent in cutting cross-section lines. This I had to do to acquaint myself with the nature of the land bordering the river and to select the best line for the road traces. The jungle undergrowth being very thick and the trees so tall, there is no seeing before one and consequently I had to go over every inch of the ground in order to satisfy myself as to where there were obstacles and where not."

Given the difficulties of these conditions, Swettenham decided that, in the interests of economy and speed, the best course was first to cut a number of rough six-feet-wide bridle-paths to link the main settlements, the mining-camps and the rivers. To hack these paths out of the jungle without the aid of any form of modern machinery was a time-consuming, labour-consuming process, as is clear from the description of Ambrose Rathborne, an ex-coffee planter who had turned his hand to road-making. Once the surveyors had laid the traces, "the undergrowth was cut down and thrown to one side, then the smaller trees were uprooted and the larger ones dug round about so as to expose their roots some little distance below the ground before being cut so that no roots should remain in the roadway . . . The heavy tops of the larger trees saved much axe work but even then it was often a *week* before two men were able to cut through sufficient roots to cause the tree to fall." Even with the expenses of two men per uprooted tree per week, Swettenham reported that most of the bridle-paths were made at the cost of only £150 per mile – each cent of which had to be convincingly accounted for when Swettenham's eagle eye combed the costings. Those submitted for one stretch of the first main road between Kuala Lumpur and Klang included sums for coolies', overseers', blacksmiths' and bullock-keepers' wages; for charcoal for the blacksmith's smithy; for crowbars, baskets and picks; for stanchions and piles for the first bridge; for rope for the bullocks' tethers, attap for the bullocks' sheds; for rice and medicines for sick bullocks.

Once these first thoroughfares became familiar and passable in most weathers, a number of traders emerged from the interiors and set up little thatch huts and stalls selling jungle fruits to the increasing numbers of passers-by – coolies carrying bundles of firewood, policemen, miners, revenue collectors, Chinese salesmen with baskets of calicoes and chintzes, and troupes of players, carrying hollow drums and pipes, the women dressed in colourful robes and with long gold fingernails, bound for some village festival. When the volume of traffic became sufficiently great to justify the expense, stretches of the paths were made wide enough for bullock-carts which carried food, timber and charcoal to the camps and tin from the mines to the river outlets.

Bullock-carts were already the main form of transport in Kuala Lumpur itself and, by the end of 1883, seventy-five were registered as "hackney carriages" for the town and duly equipped with licensing badges, oil-lamps and plates stating fixed fares. There were also twenty-two licensed pony-carts, six of the smartest belonging to Yap Ah Loy, but they were of little use beyond the town boundaries. New regulations were enforced to control all this traffic – and to limit the letting off of firecrackers in the streets and the dumping of refuse in the re-built drains.

The officers of the Public Works Department, galvanized into unwonted activity after Douglas' departure, were charged with the measuring and pegging out of saleable plots in the central district; with the pulling down of some of the old huddled-together thatch dwellings to minimize the fire hazards; with the improvement of the water supply – for people had been in the habit of bathing in the drinking-wells. Swettenham also issued instructions to clear the streams above the nearby mining-camps, to get some decent rattan couches, commodes and finger-glasses into the Rest House, to put in a pantry near the Residency dining-room, to pull down the old slaughter houses and relocate them in a remote and salubrious spot, and to clean up the brothels – which were reported to be "as filthy as pig sties" and so dark that lamps burned inside them all day. And something had to be done quickly about the main market which stood on land owned by Yap Ah Loy. Swettenham reported that it consisted of "a tumble-down shed under which is sold the produce brought in every day from the country – meat, poultry, vegetables, everything needed for daily consumption in the native town. The filth of this market is indescribable and so is the stench. Everything that rots or becomes putrid, all offal and refuse, is thrown on the ground or into the two ditches which surround the shed." Close by was the main gambling booth where business boomed day and night, and Swettenham was soon at loggerheads with Yap Ah Loy over this because he wanted to have it moved on the grounds that "such sights in such a central location have a demoralizing effect on the populace".

Swettenham's driving initiative was soon appreciated by Weld who, after he had been only three months in office, minuted the Colonial Office that the new Resident "has found things in a disgraceful state and has a great work before him which he is energetically and ably undertaking and will no doubt carry through with success". But not even one of Swettenham's calibre could accomplish everything single-handed and, as he himself wrote, it was at that time very difficult to attract sufficient men "prepared for the hardest work under conditions that could not be expected to appeal to any but the few ready to sacrifice everything for the pleasure of taking part in a great adventure".

Working days were long – no more rolling in at eleven o'clock; working conditions were makeshift and spartan, with nothing much in the way of cooling fans or punkahs or comfortable office furniture; nor were there any of the "civilized Europeans' customary delights", which Swettenham listed as "food, society, literature and amusement". Salaries were just adequate, mainly because there was very little to spend money on, for, in the evenings, an exhausted official had nothing to do but write up his detailed journal of the day's activities, as specially requested by His Excellency, Governor Weld, crawl under his mosquito net and dream, perchance, of home.

The rewards of the life were, as Swettenham says, those of the pioneer adventurer: constructing, making waste places habitable, shaping the future of a landscape and its communications, and "gathering people together in the villages and persuading them to build better ones". For the early Residents were not deskbound officials issuing orders to subordinates and getting no nearer the grass-roots than a game of croquet on the Residency lawn; they had to initiate, personally oversee and follow through; everyone turned to them for decisions, permissions, consultations, and the range of their authority was wide and undefined.

"A priestly officer called on me," Swettenham noted, "and wanted to find out if I had any objection to his publicly notifying in the mosque that he would neither marry nor bury those who failed to attend the mosque on Fridays when they had nothing pressing on hand to attend to." Next there came an officer to report on the sorry condition of the village Pulo Angsa which had been allowed "to spring up in an irregular fashion with the result that the shops and houses are huddled together higgledy-piggledy – and being a fishing village, the place is not clean." Attracted by the mess, crocodiles infested the river alongside the houses, and might the officer post notices offering rewards for any of the fearsome reptiles brought dead or alive to his office?

The next day Swettenham made an inspection tour of the town. He went first to the prison, to check that the prisoners had facilities for "a soap and water bath at least every second day", to reprimand a policeman caught gambling, to interview a Portuguese applying for the chief warden's post, to advise on the building of a more spacious abode for Mr Harry Syers, who had now been appointed Chief of Police in Kuala Lumpur and was about to get married – Swettenham minuted "I fear the quarters as at present constructed are not suitable for the accommodation of a lady." Then to the hospital, to check on supplies of bedding,

71

on the efficiency of a new half-caste apothecary, on the construction of a private bathroom for the surgeon, whose predecessor had recently been fired for drunkenness. And he went to see how the construction of the new brick-built treasury was progressing – for solid brick buildings were a symbol of hard-edged prosperity and permanence among all that soft, flimsy thatch, rattan and bamboo that was so easily destroyed by fire, storm, white ants. In 1883 a new brick-kiln was opened and within a twelvemonth there were ten brick buildings in the town, among them a sturdy Tin Weighing Office; three years later there were fifty-three such edifices, many of them standing along widened surfaced streets bordered with efficient monsoon drains.

For Westerners with a little capital, expertise and enterprise there were plenty of opportunities to cash in on Selangor's development. Swettenham mentions the usefulness of two or three ex-planters like Ambrose Rathborne who left the uncertainties of pioneering plantation agriculture for the sure contracts of the government's various construction programmes. Another useful arrival was John Pickersgill Rodger who had a flair for travelling, languages and law and was soon appointed Chief Magistrate (and later became a Resident of Selangor in his turn). And there was William Cameron from Singapore, brother of the editor of the *Straits Times*. A quiet and cultured amateur geologist, he used to take off into the hinterlands for weeks on end accompanied only by an aboriginal guide. He mapped out the high tableland on the Perak–Pahang borders known since as the Cameron Highlands and used to return to Kuala Lumpur at unpredictable intervals bringing samples of unexploited mineral deposits. But the isolation and hardship apparently proved too much for him and, says Swettenham, he was "subject to delusions". Once while staying in the Kuala Lumpur Residency Cameron took a pot shot at his Chinese servant and, Swettenham adds, "when I went to his room and told him I had removed all his firearms because of that incident, he merely remarked, 'Yes, but I didn't hit him.'"

Qualified engineers were at a premium in Selangor at the time and one of the first on the scene was Spence-Moss, who headed a railway construction team lent by the Ceylon Government. Swettenham was very keen to get a railway linking Kuala Lumpur with the port of Klang, even though he estimated that its construction would cost about twice as much as Selangor's entire annual revenue. The Straits Settlements Government lent half the sum required and the rest had to be financed as the work progressed from the State's funds, mainly the tin-mining revenue. It was a gamble, but one that paid off handsomely – in Swettenham's view at least. He reported that as soon as the railway was opened, receipts so far exceeded the working expenses that within a year the line earned a profit equal to twenty-five per cent on the capital expended. "It may be questioned whether that record has ever been equalled in railway building," he concludes, with his customary modesty.

The historic railway was opened in 1886 with much ceremony and a flourish of inaugural speeches. The leader of the Malay community claimed that "since the arrival of the British Resident in this country we have felt as one lifted up and placed between earth and sky, so great has been the change from our previous to our present conditions." Sir Frederick Weld came up from Singapore and the ancient Sultan Abdul Samad, who had not left Langat for the previous six years, was prevailed upon to come as well. He was awarded a K.C.M.G. for his pains and a ride with Weld in the first train, on which occasion he was reported to have remarked to the Governor that this novel conveyance was the best bullock-cart he had ever travelled in.

A wily bird, Abdul Samad, who had perforce lived to see a lot of changes in the twelve years since the young Frank Swettenham had first stalked into Langat and started "advising" him on how to administer his realm. The Sultan had contrived to remain on pretty good terms with practically all the strangers he had seen since – the pushy Swettenham, the solitary English lady who used to walk in daily boredom along his village mud path, the various Governors, Residents, snipe-shooters, prospectors and tax collectors who steamed up the Langat river from time to time. He had smiled kindly upon them all and agreed with them – in theory if not in practice – while steering clear of political controversy and the wiles of his waiting heirs. He was in his seventies when he bumped along with Weld in that steam-driven bullock-cart, but he still had several years to live and many changes to see, for the uneventful tropical routines of his youth had gone for ever, and nothing stood still for long in Malaya anymore.

7

The Ruler into the fold

To have had experience of any formerly uncharted terrain for as long as ten years is, in the beginning, to be an old hand; one upon whom newcomers can rely to provide tangible evidence of survival, to dispel fears of the unknown, to crystallize recent adventure into the security of past history. So Hugh Charles Clifford, a new cadet in the Perak Service, posted to the Kuala Kangsa Residency in 1884 when he was nineteen years old, regarded Frank Swettenham, the Acting Resident of Perak during Low's home leave, as a man of vast and valuable experience. The presence of Clifford and another young cadet, Martin Lister, "added immensely to the pleasure of a life full of interest and varied incident", wrote Swettenham. "Poling or paddling a dugout, swimming in the clear waters of the river were our chief recreation; but there was so much work to be done that there was seldom time for mere joy" ... a typical comment of a born workaholic.

Clifford was another man capable of much dogged hard work, but he lacked Swettenham's self-assured grasp of reality and sense of rightness, possessing instead a sensitivity of thought, a breadth of imagination that later led him toward uncertainty. He was athletic, tall and strong-looking, but he suffered more than his share of the white man's disorders in the East – headaches, insomnia, skin rashes and stomach upsets. His quiet and courtly manner suggested his origins, for he sprang from one of the most notable Roman Catholic landed families in England and had been privately educated during a sheltered childhood in the formerly Royalist manors of the West Country, where the Cliffords had been ensconced for centuries. His father was a major-general and Hugh, after passing his entrance for Sandhurst, had intended to follow in his footsteps; but he suddenly decided to join the Malay Civil Service instead, perhaps partly because Sir Frederick Weld was his father's cousin.

Weld gave his young relative every opportunity to learn the ropes well, first from Swettenham and then from Hugh Low when he returned to Perak. In this way Clifford gained the beginnings of that understanding of Malay life and language and a sympathetic liking for the people which were to be of decisive influence in his later life. He also picked up the rudiments of the various skills – such as the interpretation of surveyors' and collectors' reports, the diplomatic dealing with local deputations, the assessment of expenditure estimates – which were all in the day's Residential work.

Early in 1887 Weld decided that young Clifford was capable of his first solo assignment and he was instructed to accompany one Raja Muda to the east coast state of Pahang. The assignment was solo and very tricky. Pahang was, at that time, Malaya's most isolated state, very difficult of access by land from the west, and cut off from all sea communication during most of the autumn and winter when the monsoons swept fiercely in from the China Sea. Because of its inaccessibility and its inhabitants' reputation for proud and violent isolationism, Pahang had so far remained more or less unaffected by the British presence in the Peninsula.

Foreigners had penetrated there of course – intrepid naturalists and planters, one or two diplomatic missions and engineers in search of mining concessions, for the ruler of Pahang was in the habit of selling large tracts of land to the highest bidders, even though they had been mined by small local companies for years. Swettenham had long been interested in Pahang's development and in 1885 had made an exploratory journey of 402 miles by river to Pekan, its capital on the South China Sea. It was a spectacular and exciting trip – particularly the shooting of numerous rapids aboard bamboo rafts which had two polers, fore and aft, and two passengers who clung tightly to the raised central platform. What with the delays and hazards of the rapids, of fallen trees and snags in the river, and the scarcity of boatmen, their average speed was about fifteen miles per day. At night, they stopped at villages along the rivers where the headmen all complained of the unsettled state of the countryside and the ruinous taxes imposed by the Sultan and his chiefs. Arriving in Pekan, the expedition moored their rafts opposite the mosque and were hospitably received by the Sultan. But, on the whole, the place was "unregenerate", Swettenham decided. By this he meant that it had not yet been regenerated by the forward march of Western progress: it was "a mass of undeveloped jungle without a mile of road anywhere" and "the present occupation of the ruling class was top-spinning".

However, because of Pahang's "size and geographical position it was important to get its Ruler into the fold – a position he was not at all eager to occupy for he had never known control of any kind", Swettenham explained. "Getting the Ruler into the fold" was a cosy euphemism for the brand of ambitious expansionism favoured by Governor Weld, who was determined to bring Pahang within the Residential system in the interests of administrative tidiness, strategic advantage and economic potential, for it was reputed to contain vast untapped timber and mineral reserves. Also, Weld believed that the Pahangese, being Asiatics, could never really govern themselves. It was "contrary to the genius of the race, of their history, of their religious systems that they should. Their desire is a mild, just and firm despotism that we can give them," he wrote confidently to the Colonial Office.

A handy tool for giving the Pahangese what was best for them was Raja Muda, an heir apparent and brother of the ruling Sultan, who, since his last unsuccessful bid for power, had been living in exile. For Pahang had long been beset by factional conflicts, and its people, wrote Hugh Clifford, "think chiefly of deeds of arms, of illicit love intrigues and the sports which their religion holds to be sinful". Cock-fighters, gamblers and brawlers, the males were "exceedingly touchy and quick to take offence" – also loyal, cheery, hardworking when necessary and fond of cutting a dash. Thus the State's royal family, presumably typical of their kind, quarrelled more violently and frequently than most and when, in an earlier period of temporary reconciliation, Swettenham had again gone to Pahang on a similar mission to Clifford's, he found that the Sultan "was unkindly described as the wickedest man in Asia". This, Swettenham says, he was not; but he certainly strongly resisted the British efforts to intervene in his realm's affairs, and vowed that "as long as we and our children are still living" there would not be a British administration in Pekan.

An imperialist less dogged than Weld might have left it there, but he, according to a modern historian, "badly needed the planting of the British flag on Pahang's soil if his image as a great pioneer of Empire was to be restored before he retired, which was soon". In that cause, Weld himself paid a visit to Pekan in 1886, accompanied by Hugh Low and Hugh Clifford, in an effort to persuade the Sultan to accept just one little in-offensive British Agent who would softly, softly "mediate and appease enmities ... keep the Governor well informed, doing nothing of consequence except after reference to him". When Weld and his entourage arrived they were kept waiting for several hours on the river-bank while the Sultan finished a game of chance with a Chinese friend. When they were eventually granted an audience, the Ruler expressed his complete disinterest in the British proposals – mindful, perhaps, of the old Malay proverb, "When the needle is in, the thread is sure to follow." Weld left empty-handed and baffled, but not defeated.

The following year therefore, when Raja Muda was returning to Pahang after a second period of exile, Weld sent with him Hugh Clifford, whose instructions were clear: "I wish to obtain an agreement or a convention of amity," Weld told him. "It would be a great gain if we could obtain a written undertaking that no convention should be made with foreign powers by Pahang except through the Governor, next to that, that no concessions should be granted except in this way." And so the twenty-year-old Clifford set off for Pahang, full of confidence and excitement, in a steam-yacht called *Will o' the Wisp*, with Raja Muda, his nephew and two holy men. When the rivers became unnavigable, the procession cut across country – sixteen coolies and several elephants loaded with the Raja's boxes and bundles, food supplies and diplomatic gifts. Along the whole route drums and gongs were sounded ahead to alert any existing populace of their important passing.

Life in rural Malaya fired Clifford's imagination from the start. The country became his most absorbing interest for the next sixteen years; he retained an emotional identification with it long after he had left its shores; in the course of his life he wrote more than eighty stories and essays on the theme. Many of his best writings were inspired by his early experiences in Pahang, when, as the only official British resident there, he found himself entirely at the mercy of the country for sustenance, companionship and joy.

One of the first joys was the pristine beauty of the land itself, as seen from some small native craft in which "you can almost fancy yourself one of the early explorers skirting the lovely shores of some undiscovered country. As you sprawl on the bamboo deck under the shadow of an immense palm-leaf sail . . . you look out through half-closed lids on the beautiful coast . . . Waves dance and glimmer and shine in the sunlight, the long stretch of sand is yellow as a buttercup and fringes of graceful casuarina trees quiver like aspens in the breeze and shiver in the heat haze . . . As you glide through cluster after cluster of thickly wooded islands, you lie in that delightfully comatose state in which you have all the pleasure of existence with none of the labour."

Once landed however, Clifford was soon jolted into working reality, for, as Weld had put it in a dispatch to the Colonial Office, forestalling any suggestion of nepotism, "It is no pleasure post in which I have placed my relative. Rice and dry fish to eat, no European to consult with, and obliged to sit up night after night till dawn in crowded houses at Court in the tropical heat . . ." In one of his early stories, which is a barely fictionalized account of his experiences in Pahang and the events which led to its eventual shepherding into the Residential fold, Clifford describes his mode of living in Pekan which bears out Weld's picture.

The place itself was little more than an enlarged village with only four substantial buildings – two of them mosques. Most of the trade was local and the great majority of the inhabitants had travelled but little in their lives and regarded Clifford with suspicion and some slight contempt. He was quartered in a rambling thatch dwelling, part of which abutted on the main street and ". . . the rest of the premises straggled out over the river on half a hundred crazy wooden piles". The main reception room contained a raised platform where Clifford ate his daily bowls of rice and fish and received visitors. He spent most of his time in a small oblong room built over the water. Its furnishings were not elaborate. The plank floor was covered with a straw mat; there were a few large pillows for sleeping, a green earthenware jar for his cigarette ends, some books in Arabic, two cane chairs and a leather portmanteau containing his clothes.

During the day, the river below flashed whitely in the strong sun, its shadows rippling on the woven walls, its waves lapping against the ladder leading to the bathing-raft when some slim craft drifted by. Sometimes, the waters were more deeply disturbed by the arrival of a Chinese trading junk, smelling of spices and dried fish, "a huge, round-bellied, blunt-nosed affair with a knowing looking fish's eye on either side of the prow, such as had crept up and down the seas of south-eastern Asia any time during the past five thousand years". In the early evenings, one or two of Clifford's retinue came to squat on the floor of the room, "chewing quids of areca nut and talking together in low murmurs. Through the narrow slits of window, the moonbeams strove to penetrate in defiance of the greasy lamplight, and the insistent hum of insects, varied by the occasional note of the night-jar, was borne upon the almost motionless hot air."

Later, Clifford would saunter along to the store of a Chinese trader who, when he arrived, would usually be filling a long bamboo pipe with opium "which he was toasting at the end of a slim steel skewer over the small lamp which stood on the mat beside him. The faint smell of the drug filled the room as the opium swelled into big brown blisters or subsided like a bubble as it was cooked." In this "sufficiently squalid place" and the

nearby Hall of State – an open-sided shed adjacent to the Royal
Palace where the Chinese merchants spread their gambling mats
– the gentry of Pekan gathered to gossip until the early hours, and
Clifford, whose business it was to learn all he could about local
affairs, would gossip too, and drink tea, chew coconut and sugar
sweetmeats and make mental notes for later forwarding to the
Singapore Secretariat.

During one such night, after Clifford had been waiting around
in the Pahang capital for nearly four months gently trying to
convince the Sultan that he should do as the British wanted, he
noted in his journal that "His Highness came out to see me at
3 a.m. and was very cordial and nice . . . He led me into a separate
room. Here he gave me a letter he had prepared . . . and asked
me to read it. I did so and saw at a glance that he therein asked
for a treaty with the English government . . . It has evidently been
written against his wish and he was almost in tears. I then thanked
and congratulated His Highness as warmly as I could . . ."

Clifford was cock-a-hoop and rushed back to Singapore to
report to Weld, feeling himself by far the cleverest young diplomat in the Service – though he was realistic enough to add that the
success of his mission was mainly due to the pressure brought to bear
on the Sultan by a strong party of chiefs from Johore, to which
Pahang was closely allied. Weld was enormously pleased that his
relative had proved to be a most promising chip off the old block,
having succeeded "by the exercise of all those qualities that mark
a man out as exceptionally fitted to manage native races".

Ever the optimist, Weld reported to the Colonial Office that
"our relations with Pahang promise to be put shortly on a basis
of permanent friendship". He added confidently that, in Clifford's
view, "the great preponderance of feeling amongst the chiefs
and almost universal feeling amongst the people is in favour of
British influence, even to the full establishment of the full Residential system – and no wonder, for they hear of the good
government of the Protected States and know that there the
people are free from oppression and that the chiefs get regular
allowances, whereas in Pahang there is neither law nor justice
and assassination is the usual procedure by which administrative

and financial questions are dealt with." From the Made-in-Britain cornucopia of imperial benefits it was, of course, "the Natives themselves who will be the greatest gainers".

Clifford was soon to revise his over-sanguine early estimate of the situation in Pahang and in the event the British advance there was not that smooth. After the initial breakthrough, there followed a great deal of what one Colonial Office official termed "unnecessary, hampering and aimless, self-important, secret, quasi-diplomatic bother", during which the reluctant Sultan did several about-turns, Clifford charged back and forth between Pekan and Singapore, and the Colonial Office began to complain of Weld's "hot-headed impetuosity" in trying to force the issue through at all. "If we enter on a general crusade in this region, where will it all end?" asked one senior Colonial Office man fretfully, perhaps realizing that the only result of the annexation of Pahang from his point of view would be an increase of paper-work and of remote-control decision-making.

Nevertheless, Weld's policy, which became known as the British Forward Movement, carried the day. On 10th October 1887, the day before he left the Straits Settlements on his retirement, Weld signed the agreement, also ratified by the Sultan, which allowed for the appointment of a British Agent in Pahang, and he wrote triumphantly to the Colonial Office in his last dispatch from the East that "our position will be much strengthened by the weight that the Malays attach to the fact that the Sultan of Pahang had made reparation and now the whole Peninsula from the countries where Siam claims sovereignty is under our influence".

The duties of the British Agent were at first limited to those of a consular officer, charged with the additional task of persuading the Sultan generally to clean up his administration. Hugh Clifford, as the only member of the Service with any real experience of the State, was the natural choice for the post; and so, in the autumn of 1887, he returned to Pekan with instructions to stay there as long as he felt advisable and to gain the Sultan's confidence in every possible way. He was vested with a little more authority than formerly, but was powerless to initiate policies or bring about administrative change. Moreover, the Sultan was not a comfortable man to deal with. He was "one of the most picturesque figures in Asia", Clifford decided. "In his youth he was a mighty warrior and to the end of his days he was a keen sportsman." The very force of his personality "claimed the tribute of a reluctant admiration", but he governed with selfish ruthlessness and "so impressed his will upon his subjects that, for them, his lightest word, his merest whim, his hinted desire were law".

Clifford recorded that the Sultan was surrounded by a privileged group of King's Youths, dressed in brilliant silks, who followed him everywhere, "to guard him from harm and give a finishing touch to his magnificence; they row his boat, hunt game and snare turtle-doves in his company; join with enthusiasm in any sport which, for the time, the Sultan is pleased to favour, such as kite-flying or peg-topping; carry the Sultan's messages, levy fines, murder those who have offended their master, seize the property which he covets, abduct women, spy upon chiefs, bring word to the Sultan of all it behoves him to know and never miss an opportunity to win his favour by satisfying his desires". These young men were the only form of police-force in the State, so Clifford is hardly exaggerating when he writes that "a political Agent left to hang around" in the atmosphere of such an oriental court on the edge of nowhere and "totally unsupported by even the show of force, has his back to the wall as a more or less permanent arrangement".

Another unsettling peculiarity of his unusual job was that the measuring of time, as most Westerners understood it, had no meaning in the land, and presently "it came to have hardly any significance" for Clifford either. There was an aimless disorder and tedium about the life that both disturbed and stimulated the young man's psychological and physical equilibrium. Visitors simply turned up at all hours, most of them nocturnal. "To bed at eight in the morning, up again at five p.m." he noted in his 1888 journal. "Walked round the big square ... Went to bed at 1 p.m. but could not sleep all night ... Went shooting alone and saw some peacocks ... Walked round the small square. Tungku Mahammed woke me up again in the early hours." He tried to arrange audiences with the Sultan as often as possible, he tried to work at a Malay-English dictionary on which he and Swettenham had agreed to collaborate, he read and re-read his small collection of books by Catholic writers, particularly Thomas à Kempis and Blaise Pascal whose thought greatly influenced his own contemplations on the nature of the Malay soul. For exercise, he went swimming off the raft in the river, snipe-shooting across the paddies and, in the evenings, he played billiards with "the notables of the Court".

Sometimes he went off on exploratory treks into the forests behind the coast, wading slowly up the shallow streams which served as "Nature's macadamized roads", stopping to rest and chat now and then with the people he met about the state of the rice harvest, the collection of taxes, the latest depredations of tigers or wild boars. He lived entirely on the local food – dried buffalo or monkey meat stiff as a board, mealy roots of the wild banana, sour fruits that sometimes "wring one's stomach with aches and pains", sago and coconut cakes wrapped in a leaf, fastened with a wooden skewer and called by the British "sago syllabub".

In spite of the discomforts, Clifford felt those untamed forests were "among the wonderful things of the Earth . . . The branches of the trees bound together by innumerable parasitic creepers form a green canopy overhead through which the fierce sunlight only forces a partial passage, the struggling rays flecking the trees with little splashes of light and colour . . . Everything is damp and moist and heavy. Enormous fungus growths flourish luxuriantly and over all, during the long hot hours of the day, hangs a silence as of the grave."

So he lived, feeling always rather close to unpredictable death, buoyed up by the challenge of a beautiful adventure, cast down by an underlying sense of isolation and emptiness. But withal, as he wrote in a story about a young man alone in an Eastern country in an almost identical situation, "This free, queer, utterly unconventional life has a fascination which is all its own. Each day brings a little additional knowledge of the hopes and fears, longings and desires, joys and sorrows, pains and agonies of the people among whom one's lot is cast. Every hour brings fresh insight into the mysterious workings of the minds and hearts of that very human section of our human race which ignorant English calmly class as 'niggers'. All these things came to possess a charm for him, the power of which grows apace and eats into the very marrow of the bone of the man who has once tasted this fruit of the great Tree of Knowledge."

From the first Clifford longed to "master" the subject of the Malay mind and he urged on his superiors the acceptance "of the Malay peoples as God and their climate have fashioned them". Yet he was required to fit their relaxed and graciously haphazard life-style – some aspects of which he found so seductive – into the orderly Western scheme of things for which he was the official advocate. His mental state was one of constant ambivalence. Sometimes he indulged in dreams of gypsy freedoms for himself, stirred by romantic yearnings for a simpler, feudal past: "To live in independent Malaya is to live in the Europe of the thirteenth century," he once wrote. At other times, the cruel oppressions of that same feudal society depressed him, adding to his sense of kithlessness and isolation, for he was well aware that, in the native eyes, he was an eccentric and clumsy creature of bad and unclean habits whom they could neither understand nor love.

The physical discomforts of his lonely life were comparatively easy to bear: "Good for the liver," he wrote stoically; but its other deprivations tried him sorely – never to hear good music or see a fine picture or "listen lovingly to conversation which strikes answering sparks from a sodden brain"; above all, never "to encounter the softening influence of the society of ladies of his own race . . ." In later years Clifford had a reputation for being something of a "ladies' man", and it must have been difficult for one so constituted to live thus bereft in his early twenties. Certainly he was well aware of the physical presence of young native women with their "downy" or "golden" skins, their large soft eyes and glossy black hair and in his stories he refers to the importance and power of sexuality. Probably he had a native mistress; it has been suggested that the mental imbalance which

85

later dogged him was a result of syphilis contracted in Pahang at this time. On such subjects the official records are silent.

Certainly in the summer of 1888 he contracted dysentery and his journal entries become sparse and pathetic: "Very seedy with the old agonies strong upon me ... No one near me all day. Can't eat or sleep and stool all the time ... Bad night again and weaker yet, can scarcely walk; must try to get to Singapore ..." He was carried aboard a Singapore-bound boat on 6th August and spent a couple of months there trying to recuperate. But his health was temporarily broken and he returned to Pekan only long enough to pack up his makeshift abode and prepare for the arrival of the first fully-fledged British Resident to Pahang – John Pickersgill Rodger from Selangor. For the Sultan had eventually been forced to accept the "advice and services" of a Resident after a series of not very scrupulous stratagems by the British who, having gained from optimists like Swettenham and Weld an over-rosy view of the State's economic potential, were determined to develop its resources under conditions of improved political stability.

While Rodger and his small staff soon "became busily engaged in the two most characteristic British duties: the raising of revenue and the writing of reports", as one historian slyly puts it, Hugh Clifford's final journal entries for that year of 1888 contrast oddly with what went before: "Charing Cross Hotel, November 13th; Mother and Harry to meet me. Met Sybil at King's Cross. Lunched with the Ribblesdales ... Dined at the Army and Navy Club with Major Younger ..." Then he sums up the previous twelve months in his usual conscientious and honest fashion as "one of the more unsatisfactory years. Very trying work in Pahang and breakdown of health under dysentery are the chief features of an unpleasing kind. The final settlement of Pahang difficulties and my return to Europe are its pleasant events."

8

"Changing the face of the land"

When Sir Frederick Weld visited Hugh Low in 1880 he described his work with great approval adding that "the Resident is a man after my own heart . . . a noble fellow with a true sense of duty – an Englishman of the best type". This unstinted praise from his superior ushered in the decade which was the apogee of Low's career, and the Residency at Kuala Kangsa was its fruit and fitting symbol. All who visited the place commented favourably on its ambience of orderly calm, its sense of harmonious adjustment to the local scene. And all were impressed with the powerful personality of Low himself, who had seemingly acquired, during his long years of isolated endeavour, an humane sympathy of spirit that warmed all who met him.

One of the few European travellers to stray so far into the hinterlands was a Frenchman, M. Brau de Saint-Pol Lias, who remarked that Low's very presence – his keen glance, his venerable grey beard, the size of his figure draped in the long loose-sleeved Chinese-style robe which he wore indoors – commanded one's respectful attention. After the first evening spent listening to details of Low's past, the problems and achievements of his present, the Frenchman felt that he "had much to learn at his school".

Discipline was of its essence, though not of the rigid and rebarbative Douglas variety. In Low's fairly considerable establishment every man knew his place, and its everyday functioning was carried on with a certain stately efficiency. The major domo was, according to Lias, "a big, fat, black Klinn"; there were two valets, twins from Java; two Chinese, one a cook, the other a sweeper; one Malay punkah puller; three Sikhs who stood guard in the house day and night armed only with malacca canes which they raised in solemn salute when the Resident or his guests passed them. Gardeners, stable boys and water-carriers worked in the extensive grounds where Low kept numbers of sheep, cows imported from India and turkeys from Malacca. There was a pond for the fish caught in the nearby river and a caged Argus pheasant that was tame enough to eat corn from the hand.

Low's personal expenditure on all this was considerable, indeed he used to claim that it took most of his salary, but as a result his table was celebrated as one of the best in the Protected States. Emily Innes, who spent the Christmas of 1880 at Kuala Kangsa after her husband had been moved to Durian Sabatang in Perak, recorded that she was "astonished by the luxurious fare the Resident set before us. Fresh fish, fresh beef, fresh game, mutton and venison, preserved *pâtés de foie gras* and other luxuries from Crosse & Blackwells, iced champagne and all manner of cool drinks, made it difficult to believe that we were in the heart of the Malayan jungle." Her tone is acidulous – compare all that, she is suggesting, with the occasional scrawny jungle fowl and muddy-flavoured river fish which were *our* staple fare in the out-stations!

The Residency grounds also gave Low scope for his practical and experimental botanical interests. "No luxury, nothing for the eyes, but what interesting ideas!" wrote Lias when he saw them. "Coffee bushes from Liberia filling the air with the perfume of their white flowers as odoriferous as that of an orange flower, they are already full of berries, green and red, which allow the sowing of seedlings on a large scale. Today Mr Low has enough to plant 5,000 stems. They are the prettiest small trees one could wish to see, of a dark green large foliage and white and red fruits forming a very regular cone." Quantities of produce flourished under Low's care. Lias noticed also, "tomatoes of the most luscious red" and, most splendid of all, the pink pineapple with leaves "which redden around the fruit . . . as if in radiant continuation of its own colour; the fruit itself is marvellous, forty centimetres high, perhaps, it is surrounded at birth by a quantity of small fruits that form a crown at its base".

Low also made a point of collecting and propagating rare

species of plants and trees in the grounds, among them the famous tropical creeper *ara*, of sinister disposition. This creeper, explained Lias, "builds its gigantic trunk around the trunk of another big tree which it stifles and then substitutes itself for in such a way that one would never suspect the first tree had ever existed, had not one seen this vegetal drama reproduced constantly in the forests of this country. One can follow the adventure from the birth of the *ara* upon the bark of a *morbao* or *toualang* sometimes thirty or forty metres above ground up to the total strangling of the host tree by the roots, first thin and then enormous, which descend from the young *ara* plant, take hold on earth, thicken, multiply, and then completely trap and envelop the trunk of the first tree."

Higher in the hills, where the air was deliciously cool, Low had cleared several hectares of land for the experimental cultivation of quinine sent from Brazil, tea from Assam and Arabian coffee. And from such small beginnings developed the plantation agriculture of the Peninsula which a later historian has called, "one of the economic romances of the tropical belt". But for the pioneer planters on the spot there was very little to romanticize over and much to disappoint. Isabella Bird, for instance, mentions the arrival at Kuala Kangsa of two planters who had come "prospecting" for coffee, but were looking very "disconsolate" because Perak could offer them nothing in the way of hard-surface roads, vehicular transport, ready-cleared land or English-style houses. In such conditions one had simply to start from scratch and the life was hard, wearisome, lonely and uncertain due to the hazards of disease and financial failure.

One of the earliest and eventually most successful of the planting pioneers was that same Ambrose Rathborne who spent some time building roads in Selangor and who had left Ceylon, like several of his kind, when the coffee industry there was threatened by the spread of malignant fungus disease. The initial clearing of the land for planting released into the air such "fever-laden vapours" Rathborne claimed that many a young hopeful succumbed before the first bush even flowered. "In these parts Nature always revenges herself for being interfered with," was his explanation for such tragedies. Those who did not actually die were frequently subject to dreadful fevers which recurred for weeks on end. At such debilitating times, the poor sufferer "with emaciated body and weak tottering steps would seek a couch in the verandah in which to enjoy the deliciously fresh and cool air of the hills, until after a short while of languid but refreshing rest, a cold shivering fit would compel him to return to his bed and to cover his head and all with blankets, seeking warmth. Then followed an awful, continuous sickness, a great rise in temperature and a burning head that felt as though it were striving to split asunder, making the temples throb and ache until the consciousness that the limit of endurance was nearly reached came as a consolation and providential light-headedness supervened, giving relief from suffering."

Returned to eventual health, the planter found other problems to cope with – one of the most difficult being the acquisition of a reliable labour force. In the early 1880s, the only able-bodied men available were Malays who seldom had any wish to adapt to systematic and long-term work schedules. To persuade the men to leave the easy-going *kampong* life for the hard grind of plantation agriculture in its early stages, Rathborne paid them small advances, but, often, once these were repaid, the men "without a word would return home again". Others might stay longer, but it was all very chancy, and one brusque word or inadvertent slight would send them away for ever. The day after payday was therefore one of special anxiety, Rathborne wrote, "as to how many would remain, for a great exodus invariably occurred and there was a scarcity of labourers for the next few days till more arrived".

The first task to which the men were set was the simple and indiscriminate felling of all growth – huge and potentially valuable trees, undergrowth and creepers; then, when the timber was sufficiently dry, whole hillsides were fired. It was exciting to watch, Rathborne reported, as several men with torches began "lighting the fallen timber at the top and clambering down the hill setting light to different places as they pass and shouting as the dried wood ignites". It was a dangerous business, for if they slipped and hurt themselves, the flames would catch up with them in no time, but "a glorious sight to see the whole hillside ablaze and the fire and sparks leaping up whilst listening to the roar and crackle of the flames . . . and for days afterwards the embers glow and simmer".

In such dramatic ways did the foreigners change the face of the land – felling, burning, blazing new trails and planting out the rows of tea, sugar, tapioca, coffee, "the implementation of the cheap breakfast concept", as one wag put it. Another, angrier, writer pointed out that the customary interests of the native agriculturist and his traditional patterns of cultivation were drastically changed and superseded by large-scale plantation agriculture, and that the export-orientated system introduced by the British to "serve their own economic and political objectives" soon demanded large imports of capital and foreign expertise and a complex organization of labour use which was quite alien to the country.

In the past, rice and other staples were grown on small units of land clustered around each village and worked by separate families, and it was difficult to convince such people to cultivate more than they needed for themselves each year. Some of the small-holdings went in for gambier, sugar and tapioca, most of them run by the Chinese who were always resourceful and thrifty in their use of land resources. Gambier, which was used for tanning leather and as a medicament for dysentery, was grown in pepper plantations because its bushes supported the pepper vines and its leaves manured the soil. The growing of tapioca was combined with the rearing of pigs because the animals were fed from the waste that came from the primitive processing factories where the tapioca was soaked, pulped, strained, dried and broken into flakes.

Among the early Residents, only Hugh Clifford suggested that the introduction of large-scale plantations would cause social and economic dislocation of closely-knit and effective agricultural patterns such as these. The other British administrators were enthusiastic advocates of the new system and pointed to its successful development in other colonies in the West Indies and Africa. They believed that the combination of fertile tropical soils with European capital, drive and know-how would create a boom from which both the country and foreign investors would benefit, and that the diversification of produce would provide a cushion against depression. Moreover, both Swettenham and Low disliked the short-term and essentially destructive nature of the tin industry. "We give to the miner what is often fine land covered with magnificent forest and when he has destroyed the timber he turns the soil upside down and after a few years abandons it, leaving huge stretches of country a sightless waste of water-holes," wrote Swettenham, a "rural-Malay" man.

So the British, with all these considerations in mind, offered every encouragement to the planters who ventured into the Peninsula – in the form of loans and very favourable 999-year leases which they could purchase at very low prices. The terms of these leases were among those drawn up by William Maxwell when he was Assistant Resident under Low and they were so remarkably flexible and generous that it was surprising more foreign enterprises did not take them up. Among the chief takers were Ambrose Rathborne and his partner Heslop Hill whose names figure prominently in the Agricultural Concessions Lists of the 1880s, and who acquired 8,000 acres of land in Selangor almost rent free and 12,000 more in Perak at fifty cents an acre and no rent.

But the more land they owned, the more difficult it became to develop and the rate of actual production remained very unsatisfactory. In the mid-1880s Rathborne wrote that the "coffee bushes on the hills were beginning to repay all the trouble and labour bestowed upon them by their vigorous growth . . . fevers became less prevalent, good houses had been erected for the labourers". But there were no labourers to fill them, for the Malays were still unwilling to leave their customary pursuits and the Chinese preferred the hubbub, risk and quick returns of the mines. According to Rathborne, the estates had been opened on the understanding that Tamil labour from India would be allowed in before the first crops were ready to harvest. But, alas, "the coffee trees commenced to bean and the beans to ripen and then to fall for want of hands to pick them, and a long stretch of 360 acres of luxuriant coffee in full beaning which had been planted and cultivated under most difficult and trying circumstances had to be abandoned" – which was why versatile and persevering fellows like Rathborne temporarily turned their hands to road-making around Kuala Lumpur instead.

However, such temporary setbacks did not destroy that early optimism of so many Europeans who assumed that soil which supported such a luxuriant wealth of natural growth must become even more fertile if it were tamed into orderly and systematic production. So beautiful and so promising it was – this dark-green and sun-gold virgin land, as the philosophically-inclined Frenchman Lias thought when, one morning at Kuala Kangsa, "after coffee which the boy left with the suitable accessories in a silver service on the table of my verandah, I went for a walk on the plateau which extends behind the house. I cannot cease to marvel at this magnificent country. From this vantage point, the eye can follow the meandering of the majestic river with all its smaller tributaries. Cattle wander in its shallows and goats and a few sheep graze here and there. Sometimes, if your eyes probe the bogs, you may see the horns and huge red nostrils of a buffalo emerge; it is bathing beatifically, while in the faraway distance a wooden bell is heard; it is a stray elephant in the jungle, peacefully eating grass.

"Still, except for the hillside where I am and where the Klinns are vigorously clearing away the summit, except for the *kampong* on the river and a few houses one may see hidden under the shade of coconut palms, all this country, covered in exuberant vegetation, humid plains, hills hidden by magnificent forests, is absolutely uninhabited, uncultivated. Millions of men could people this fertile land and change its wild vegetation into rich harvests. These plains could yield rice plantations, munificent sugarcane fields, as well as manioc and indigo; these mountains seem made for cocoa, for quinine, for the most precious, the most fruitful products." That was the typically sanguinary view of foreigners at that time, and only later trial and experience would show that the land was not quite such a bounteous tropical paradise and that its most fruitful product of all had only just been introduced upon the scene.

Later that day, after his contemplative stroll along the plateau, Lias accompanied Hugh Low on an inspection tour of the barracks of the small Kuala Kangsa garrison, which was "built on piles, a metre more or less above the ground. It stands admirably well. The cannons – two pretty pieces of steel – were ready on the floor of the barrack itself. Each man stood next to his bed in total immobility when we came up with the Resident. The Sikhs, tall and grave, with their large turbans, really have a superb and imposing physiognomy. That night we enjoyed the fresh air on the verandah after dinner in our wicker chairs . . . The butler brought the inevitable soda water, when suddenly a flash followed by an explosion shook the place. It is the cannon which, every night at nine o'clock from the barrack parade ground, advises the Malays that they might sleep in peace; they are under British protection."

Yes, the Native Malay States were under British protection and most British people concerned subscribed to the essential rightness of this arrangement, from the Residents and their superiors in the Colonial Office, to the ordinary man-about-the-jungle such as Rathborne who, in the 1895 preface of his book, describes the country as "having just emerged from a state of barbarism, slave-dealing and disorder into a prosperity under British protection that has been seldom equalled in so short a space of time". Slave-dealing was the single biggest rub to the administrators in the 1880s, for the evangelically-inspired conscience about the evils of slavery had been active in England since the beginning of the century and the British Government felt duty-bound to carry its zeal for reform into this new, benighted area.

As early as 1875 the then Secretary of State had directed that the practice "be abated with as little delay as is consistent with the necessary caution which is to be observed". When Hugh Low took over the Residency in 1877 there were estimated to be about three thousand slaves in Perak and he was well aware that his predecessor, James Birch, had been murdered principally because he had not proceeded "with the necessary caution". Low intended to do better. Firstly, he set William Maxwell the task of studying the actual framework of slavery within the state. Slaves, Maxwell found, were of two principal types: some were what might be called of the classic variety, common to many different cultures: condemned criminals, aborigines, prisoners of war, the children of older slaves; but the majority were bond-slaves or victims of a system of debt-bondage which was of Indo-Chinese origin, and not strictly in accordance with the teachings of Islam.

Bond-slaves were those who had fallen into the debt of their local chief or raja and were then bound to serve him and his household by performing all kinds of menial tasks. The men worked as boatmen, domestics, labourers in the fields; the women were cooks, child-minders, weavers of cloth and mistresses for the chiefs' male entourage. The "debts" were sometimes incurred through gambling or failure to repay loans, but often they were lost in the obscurity of past generations and could not be repaid. The slaves therefore were simply chattels in the chiefs' households – between one chief and another "the loan of a slave was like borrowing a stick", as a proverb put it.

Exactly how miserable the slave's life was depended very much on the personality of the individual chief. Sometimes they were quite well treated and felt themselves to be very much a part of the household, which offered them a degree of social protection and security in return for their labour; but they had no recourse against the cruelties of a despot. Isabella Bird quoted, for example, the story that Raja Yusuf once "poured boiling water down the back of a run-away female slave and then put a red ants' nest upon it". But for all their trials, the slaves of Malaya had never staged a revolt and the society remained devoutly hierarchical: "Whoever may be king, I'll knuckle my forehead to him" was another popular saying.

So Hugh Low designed his long-term strategy for the abolition of slavery with caution and prudence, and he described it in his journal thus: "The proper way to proceed would be to induce the chiefs to declare all children born after a certain date free and then at the same time to forbid all purchasing of slaves from outside. Give to slaves the right of purchasing their freedom at a fair price which soon so reduces the numbers that the State might, after a few years, purchase the freedom of those that would be left." Clearly, slavery was an in-built and essential part of Malay "custom", and as such should have been outside the sphere of "advice" which the British were empowered to offer the rulers; clearly too the chiefs would suffer considerable financial loss when they were compelled to release their unpaid work force and Low felt it would be unfair "not to give sufficient time for the better classes to make preparations for a measure which must cause a revolution in their domestic arrangements".

Soon, however, Low was being criticized in some quarters for foot-dragging over the slavery issue. One of his most vociferous critics was James Innes who, in 1882, had resigned from the Service and returned to England, where his wife settled down to write her forthright version of life in the Malay States. One of her conclusions, incidentally, was that "having for six years seen the system of 'Protection' at work in the country, I am inclined to think that the only persons protected by it are Her British Majesty's Residents. Everyone else in the country – native or European – is practically at their mercy. They alone are protected, even from free criticism . . ."

Innes, for his part, wrote to the *London and China Express* stating that Low had once ordered him to assist in the recapturing of runaway slaves and that warrants for the re-arrest of such slaves were presented to him to sign. Emily, who always supported her husband in print whatever her private reservations, recorded in her book that the slavery question was already a matter for dispute during that Christmas of 1880 which she and her husband spent at Kuala Kangsa eating those deliciously extravagant meals. According to her, Low's opinion was that slaves were the property of their owners, "just as much as sheep or cows". When she upheld her husband's point that one had no moral justification for making such a comparison, Low apparently retorted "half in earnest, 'You are a slave yourself you know – all married women are slaves.' 'Just so',," Emily replied. "'That is precisely how I can sympathize with other slaves.'"

It was a spirited rejoinder, but the truth was that both the Inneses had a deep sense of grievance and bitterness against all their former superiors in the Service, and no real understanding of Malay life and thought. Hugh Low had such an understanding, and by working patiently through the State Council, he gradually gained the confidence and cooperation of the people. M. de Saint-Pol Lias was present at one of the Council meetings which was held at the Taiping Residency and he gave a graphic picture of their ceremonial character and of how Low, with quiet determination, pushed through his major reforms. Raja Yusuf was late, Lias recorded, and when his boat finally arrived a detachment of two hundred red-uniformed welcoming troops was marshalled at the bottom of the Residency hill. "The Resident goes towards him and receives him amidst the troops. The music plays, the cannons thunder; it is all very solemn! The Raja and the Resident, heading the procession, climb the hill and arrive in the big room where the Council table has been prepared. They sit first, exchange compliments; the secondary councillors remain a respectful distance away on the verandah."

Among this supporting cast Lias noticed a Chinese carpenter whom he had earlier seen working about the house, but now the carpenter was a councillor who eventually took his place at the table with appropriate dignity. From his observer's chair on the verandah, Lias could see his bald head and noted that "he has taken all possible measures to reunite his two solitary strands of hair to adorn his red and chubby neck with the indispensable plait that is always required of Chinese".

The proceedings began: the Raja is in the President's seat with the Resident on his right. "But no matter where Mr Low sits," Lias commented, "it is obvious that he is the one who constantly conducts the debates and does it as a man who is perfectly used to dominating his audience." On Low's other side sat Raja Idris, Yusuf's son-in-law and heir apparent to the Perak succession. Idris was of more promising and tractable material than Yusuf, "full of good will," Lias felt, and "one of those intelligent men who may perhaps have no ideas of their own but understand only too well those of others". Low thought highly of Idris' character and abilities, using him as a moderating influence to set against Yusuf's harshness and grooming him unobtrusively for his future sultanship.

So Idris sat obediently at Low's side, wearing "a magnificent costume all of violet satin" and beaming occasionally – "wanting to show that he understands the Resident well by approving all his requests". Most of the debates usually centred on how the rules and regulations imposed by the Resident could best be fitted into the existing routines of rural Malay life and custom. For example: Was the practice of vaccination against smallpox contrary to Islamic law? Should traders be allowed to sell goods from river boats in competition with land-bound shopkeepers who had to pay the newly introduced taxes and rents? Should marriage by abduction of a girl under sixteen be a punishable offence under the new penal code?

At the meeting that Lias witnessed, the proceedings seemed to be "restricted to a complete approbation of Mr Low's opinions, if they are expressed, or a positive answer when required. Mr Low is quite good at explaining to the Council where the veritable interests of their country lie; he speaks Malay so that he can be understood by all; his tone is persuasive. If an objection occurs it is answered with good sense; if it persists at the risk of time being wasted, a suitable friendly jest is ready, a subtle sentence that assures his audience's laughter, and the incident is forgotten. The objector remains confused on the spot and does not dare say more; the Resident relieves him with a kind word." This manner of procedure was typical. A recent analysis of the workings of the Perak and Selangor State Councils of the period confirms that, as a modern historian writes, "Direct control over every aspect of the government was exercised by the Residents, with the Governor of the Straits Settlements behind them as the final source of authority, while the form and appearance of independent Malay initiative was preserved."

It was with these tactics of political cajolery allied to steely intent and backed with strong authority that Low eventually persuaded the Council members that the abolition of slavery was in the best interests of their country. It was agreed that slave-owners should receive compensation for their losses at the rate of sixty Mexican dollars for a female slave and thirty for a male, and that all outstanding sums still due on the day of emancipation would be paid by the government. On 31st December 1883 all the slaves in Perak were officially freed without any disturbance. It was a personal triumph for Low who had managed to retain the loyalty and cooperation of the chiefs while quietly keeping them out of executive positions and yet allowing them a sense of responsibility and partnership.

The remaining years of Low's Residential tenure were characterized by the same patient tenacity and practical humanitarianism. Under his guidance the economic position of Perak began to improve; there was a considerable increase in the tin revenue as the industry became more efficient and modernized. The other main source of State revenue was from the sale of licences which granted to their purchasers (usually Chinese syndicates) the exclusive right to several lucrative pursuits such as the collection of duty on firewood or jungle produce in a certain district, on the manufacture of a local heady toddy, on the operation of a town's only pawn shop.

This system of "farming" of revenues, which had been in existence before the British came, enabled whatever powers-that-were to avoid some of the trouble and expense of individual revenue collection and minimized their risk – because it was the "farmer" who had to gamble on making a large enough profit from his monopoly to compensate for the cost of the licence. Between 1885 and 1890 the receipts from tin and the licences made up about four-fifths of Perak's total revenue, which was why Low was reluctant to change the system – though it did not square too comfortably with his conscience, for by far the most lucrative monopolies were those concerned with gaming and the sale of opium.

The gaming-houses, a central feature of every village street, were, wrote Ambrose Rathborne, "a most pernicious and demoralizing influence; they openly entice the passer-by to try his luck and allure the weak-minded to their ruin as well as being a fruitful source of misery and crime". He continued with a vivid picture of the "haggard and dubious" faces of the miners clustered anxiously round the tables in the hot, noisy dens. These men were ignorant, poor and uneducated, Rathborne pointed out, and "the direct encouragement of this vice is most discreditable to the British administration". In reply to this kind of criticism, Swettenham, ever the apologist for British policies, wrote that the Chinese had always been inveterate gamblers anyway and so, for "the miners living in the jungle with no source of amusement open to them and plenty of time on their hands, no power short of an incorruptible police constable attached day and night to each Chinese could stop it". A similarly pragmatic argument was put forward in the case of opium-smoking – another inveterate habit among the Chinese mining community. This meant, of course, that the expansion of the tin industry had the satisfactory corollary of increasing the amount of duty that the government collected from the growing opium consumption.

Though the State was becoming more prosperous, Low was no less thrifty and he was constantly concerned to ensure that government funds were deployed prudently. His monthly circulars, distributed to all his staff, contained stern admonitions on such matters as "More Economy in the Use of Stationery", with suggestions on using half-sheets to reduce bulk. The same document queried the heavy expense of overland and water transport of Council members to their meetings and the recent requests from some of his own officers who wanted their salaries increased to the level paid to similar functionaries in other States. "It never seems to occur to anyone to reduce a salary to that paid for similar work elsewhere," Low comments drily.

His approach to the use of natural resources was equally provident, and Perak was the first state to issue regulations governing the conservation of water supplies, jungle woods and wildlife. A circular of 1888 states that, from 4th July onward, no mangrove trees would be cut down of "a smaller diameter than three inches inside the bark at three feet from the ground". It is rather hard to imagine charcoal burners and woodcutters armed with rulers making the requisite measurements – but Low warned that heavy fines would be imposed on any transgressors of the new rule. Similar fines would be imposed on those who unlawfully set traps in the rivers for the turtles during the off-season and it was one of the many duties of the *penghulus* to remind fishermen of this.

A confirmed believer in the beauties and bounties of nature, Low remained convinced that the surest route to solvency was through more diversified agricultural production, and he continued to encourage planters to come and work in Perak in spite of the early difficulties and failures. Indeed, one of the few criticisms later levelled at him was that he allowed planters too much latitude in the selection of land and the monopolizing of water supplies. He was very enthusiastic about the growing of pepper and cinchona, and brought in some Chinese planters with the relevant experience – but their ventures did not prosper. He also encouraged the Chinese to cultivate more sugar, and in his Annual Report of 1884 he wrote, "It affords me much pleasure for the first time to include an export of 93,102 piculs of white cane sugar from the Krian district, produced on lands which, five years ago, were swampy jungle . . ."

His most spectacular horticultural triumph was the introduction, in 1877, of about a dozen unfamiliar plants sent from South America via Kew Gardens and Ceylon for experimental planting in the Residency gardens. From the first, he was excited about their potential and Frank Swettenham mentioned that when he was staying at Kuala Kangsa soon after their arrival, "Low was so keen to show me his new acquisitions that after dinner he took me into the moonlit night to point out . . . the *Hevea* seedlings in a garden on the river bank". Their full name was *Hevea Braziliensis* and two years later Low reported that they were "twelve to fourteen feet high. They take to the country immensely." The following year the first Para rubber tree to flower in the East bloomed in the Kuala Kangsa grounds and bore fruit the next season. When Low was on leave in 1885, Swettenham, as Acting Resident, supervised the collection of four hundred seeds from the first twelve trees. "Three hundred and ninety-nine germinated," Swettenham recorded. "And I had the satisfaction of planting them on the sides of a small valley at the back of the Residency."

Although the early growth of rubber trees was promising and rapid, their cultivation on any large scale remained experimental and tentative for several years because latex could not be drawn from them in profitable quantities until they were five or six years old and the planters in Malaya had little or no experience in dealing with them. Low managed to arouse some interest in their potential among a few of the planters by offering rubber seeds and plants "to any person or institution who will take care of them", but most of the planters continued to pin their hopes on coffee and other tropical products with which they were more familiar.

Nor were the Chinese interested in the new crop. Swettenham reported that he asked the prosperous Capitan China of Kuala Lumpur to open up an area for rubber cultivation, but he only smiled and replied, "Tin mining is good enough for me." There is a slight conflict of evidence here though and the enthusiasm which Swettenham expressed for rubber in his later writings might have been much fired by hindsight. For Henry Ridley, a Director of the Singapore Botanical Gardens and another early rubber enthusiast, recorded that, in 1889, when the first trees at Kuala Kangsa were tapped and the results were disappointing, Swettenham ordered the destruction of some of them and rebuked Ridley for dealing in "exotics". "It was due to Sir Frank Swettenham that Para rubber was not planted ten years earlier than it was," Ridley wrote positively.

The year 1889 was that of Low's retirement, so he was no longer on hand to protect his trees and left the country without guessing the eventual scale of the industry he had helped to initiate. In other directions his accomplishments were recognized – though he was, in a sense, too successful for his own good. When, in 1886, he had asked for advancement in the Service, the Colonial Office admitted that "his special value to Perak has militated against his promotion elsewhere". And now, "mainly on account of his age", there was "no hope of promotion to higher office".

So Hugh Low retired; a G.C.M.G. was bestowed upon him and a generous pension that enabled him to spend most of his retirement in Italy, where he died in 1905. Frank Swettenham, who was not lavish in his praise of others, wrote of Low that "It would be difficult to over-state the value of his twelve years' administration". He had, Swettenham claimed, brought peace, order and solvency to Perak and while "the many useful public works completed during the period of his office were the outward signs of his successful administration, the real value of Sir Hugh Low's work was to be found in the influence he exerted to prove

to the Malays the meaning of justice, fair dealing and a consideration for their claims, their customs and their prejudices". It was a
typically contemporary assessment made by an even more fervent
and convinced colonialist than Low was. Times change; but in
spite of all the later reappraisals, Hugh Low retains the certain
distinction of a meaningful life.

9

"*The wants of a rapidly growing administration*"

Hugh Low's retirement from Perak, the senior Residential post, caused a jockeying for position – the two main contenders being Frank Swettenham and William Maxwell. The former had the advantage of his highly successful record in Selangor during the previous seven years; Maxwell, on the other hand, had been sent to Australia by Sir Frederick Weld in 1883 to study its land conveyancing system, and had, on his return, been appointed Commissioner of Land based in Singapore. He had been charged with the task of reforming the Straits Settlements land administration – the existing state of which he characterized as "a monstrous growth resulting from the unreasoned acceptance of inapplicable theories".

Mordant comments such as this, which were indicative of his generally critical, often censorious approach to the work of his colleagues and superiors, had not made Maxwell more popular over the years. Swettenham, though equally ambitious and obstinate, was more tolerant in his attitude to others, and his wholehearted dedication to work was tempered with a certain realistic acceptance of the fact that nothing was likely to be absolutely perfect in this, or in any other part of an imperfectly-constituted world. With regard to personal relationships therefore, as well as to years of Peninsula experience, though not to seniority, Swettenham had the edge. He was also more singleminded in his determination to stay on the Malayan scene; whereas Maxwell had previously applied for posts in other colonies, partly because he had a growing family to support and was more in need of a higher salary. Anyway, Swettenham got the job and Maxwell was "given Selangor". Their direct rivalry for the post, which was common knowledge in the Singapore Secretariat, did nothing to improve their already strained relations, and each set out to prove that he was the more efficient and successful administrator, and each intended to run the affairs of his State in very much his own individual way.

In terms of purely economic progress, both Perak and Selangor forged ahead rapidly. Their total revenues and the value of exports increased dramatically, and there was a corresponding increase in the populations, predominantly due to the influx of Chinese and Indian immigrants attracted by the opportunities for employment in the tin industry and the building of roads and railways. More Europeans also arrived to administer the burgeoning bureaucracies, with the result, according to a modern historian, that "in all practical terms the Malays came to play less part in the shaping of their lives, though side by side with the Western structure of economic and administrative growth, the form and some of the substance of the pre-colonial world was preserved in sufficient degree to ensure that traditional life could, to all appearances, go on much as before".

What could not go on quite as before was the work of the Resident himself, and the days when he could sit leisurely on his verandah listening patiently to one man's tale of woe about the trampling of his paddy by a neighbour's buffalo were fast disappearing. Now, much of the rice-roots village work devolved upon the District Officers – formerly called Collectors and Magistrates – who acted as Residents-in-miniature for their territorial districts, of which there might be six or seven within a State.

Like the *penghulus*, whom he supervised, a D.O.'s duties were multifarious, most essential being the need to keep himself informed of everything going on in the native community. Clifford, in his pleasantly informal, forceful style, characterized the work thus: "He should know almost every soul in his district personally, should be so patient that he can listen unmoved to an hour's unadulterated twaddle in order that he may not miss the facts which will be contained in the three minutes' conversation which will terminate the interview. For the speech of the Oriental is like a scorpion, it carries its sting in the tail. He must above all be so thoroughly in touch with his people and his chiefs that it is impossible for any act of oppression to be perpetrated, any grievance, real or fancied, to be cherished or any trouble to be brewing without the facts coming speedily to his ears. To do this he must rival the restlessness of the Wandering Jew and must thereby so impress his people with a sense of his ubiquity that all learn to turn to him instinctively for assistance, sympathy or advice."

While the D.O.s tried to comply with fairly tall orders like this and described in copious, frequent dispatches the results of their soundings to the Residents, the latter were involved in the higher reaches of administration and legislation, the juggling of economic and personnel alternatives, the formation of long-term policy decisions. Swettenham, who moved into the Kuala Kangsa Residency to be near his friend Sultan Idris, who had duly taken over the Sultanate on Raja Yusuf's death, described *his* new duties thus: ". . . moving about the country in consultation with influential Malay chiefs, devising schemes for the construction of needed public works, especially roads, railways, water supplies, hospitals, prisons, schools and other numerous buildings which must be provided to meet the wants of a rapidly growing administration. In Perak, with its long-established and elaborate tradition of titles and offices, it was necessary to give much time and consideration to appointing the right men to fill vacancies and the settlement of disputes about allowances and determining claims to land and mines, while forms and instructions had to be prepared and issued for the guidance of practically all government officers. Legislation was dealt with by a State Council and a capable legal adviser to draft the needed measures was one of the first necessities."

Having got all this in motion, Swettenham, for once, allowed himself a little time to enjoy himself – often in the company of Sultan Idris who, after visiting England and having been long under Hugh Low's guidance, had become, in Swettenham's view, a wise, capable and tractable ruler. It was Idris who introduced Swettenham to "the amusing and exhilarating Malay game of *mêng-gêlunchor*, where the players slide down the smooth rock bed of a mountain stream to plunge into a pool at the bottom. With His Highness, his ladies and a large party of their friends, I went in gaily decorated houseboats down the Perak River to net fish in a deep backwater, and again to dig up the nests and collect the eggs of the river turtle on a great stretch of golden sand."

There were also the delights of royal fishing picnics, when the fish, after being stunned by dynamite, were caught and killed by skilful divers, "and then cooked on wood fires by the river's brink and eaten with rice and condiments. The journey through the forest was made on fifty elephants, and, when returning, the ardent spirits of both sexes indulged in a battle of jungle fruits." For this combat, the elephants were loaded with panniers of unripe fruit and four riders would take it in turns to go ahead along the track and pelt their friends with the fruit from a convenient ambush – to the accompaniment of "much laughter and considerable damage to paper sunshades used as shields". Swettenham adds that on these very informal occasions he was usually the only non-Malay present, which says much about the warmth and trust he inspired among his many native friends.

Back in his normal routine of work, the only really new item on the agenda was that of schools. In the earlier days, the British did not consider that the introduction of English-style education was very wise, for there was a widespread, if generally unspoken, fear among the authorities that too much Western-inspired knowledge might eventually prove a subversive influence. Nor was there much demand for it among rural Malays, who were suspicious of any non-Moslem culture. When Swettenham took over in Perak, he concentrated on the setting up of an elementary educational system that would "teach Malay boys their own language, give them a practical knowledge of figures and encourage them . . . to acquire information to enable them to earn a livelihood".

The learning of English, he explained, could not be widespread owing to the lack of manpower and resources, and it was therefore inadvisable "to attempt to give to the children of an agricultural population an indifferent knowledge of a language which to all but a few could only unfit them for the duties of life and make them discontented with anything like manual labour". On this issue, Maxwell's views were fairly similar. He introduced into Selangor a few provisions for giving an English-style education to the sons of rajas and chiefs – but he saw no point in emulating British educational policy in India, a country now "swarming with half-starved and discontented men who consider manual labour beneath them because they speak a little English".

At the time such views were widely held; in retrospect they have been roundly condemned as a kind of double-think which enabled colonialists to keep the natives deprived of opportunities for educational self-advancement that might have led to social discontent and political unrest, while the Europeans (and, to some extent, the Chinese) forged ahead and secured all the top managerial and professional positions. As in several other areas, British thinking on the subject was muddled and inconsistent, which allowed the administrator-on-the-spot to take initiatives or do very little as he thought fit.

By nature, neither Swettenham nor Maxwell were content to leave things as they found them, and when Maxwell took over in Kuala Lumpur he embarked on a massive reorganization of the State's land administration which was an implied criticism of his predecessor. The difference between the two men's approach to the matter centred on whether or not there was an existing custom of land tenure in Malay which was part of the Moslem religious code. If so, this should be taken very much into account in the framing of new land legislation – which, Maxwell felt, had not happened in Selangor. Swettenham doubted the relevance or even the existence of any such indigenous code. The wrangle went on for some time and was eventually submitted to the Colonial Office whose lawyers drily ruled that it was "improbable that the maxims relating to land embodied in the traditions, laws and sacred books of the Muslims and carried by them westward as far as Bosnia and south-eastwards as far at least as Malacca, should have, as it were, passed by and passed over the single state of Selangor and left no trace on the customs of the country".

Point to Maxwell; and another over the scandal of that Mr Bristow whom Swettenham had first appointed as storekeeper and later elevated to Chief Assistant of Selangor's Public Works. Maxwell, who was a diligent enquirer into the niceties of land sales to foreigners, found that Bristow had been involved in several shady speculations. Bristow absconded; Maxwell, in a dispatch, doubted the reliability of Swettenham's judgment. Moreover, Maxwell reported that, as land values around Kuala Lumpur had risen by leaps and bounds as the town developed, "Government officials of all classes have trafficked largely in land in the state of Selangor", and, "in many cases, names of officers' wives, children and other relatives crop up in the records". He added a stern warning to any who were still infringing the recognized rules of holding land or "sheltering under the names of others".

Then there was the case of Mr Spence-Moss, the railway engineer, which topped the local headlines for weeks. Moss had been asked to undertake a survey for a rail line which would link the towns of Telok Anson and Tapah. It had been a controversial project from the first and provides a fascinating example, in retrospect, of the way in which considerations of short-term expediency and long-term interest had to be weighed in the planning of new public facilities. Moss, and Swettenham who had appointed him, saw it principally in terms of engineering economics; but, in the view of the Straits Settlements Governor, the scheme was more than that. "There is no question as to the shortest route from Telok Anson to Tapah," he explained, "but rather to the direction of line which would best serve to develop the State" by passing "through excellent country already inhabited". And, His Excellency continued, "if the route runs through good country it would save expenditure on roads". But, Swettenham retorted, "even a very short distance of steep gradient on an otherwise level line means much in the working of traffic, the type of locomotive and the power to earn a fair interest on capital".

Moss disputed H.E.'s views too, saying that much of the country through which the line would pass was not at all well inhabited – reports of the abundance of rhino, Argus pheasant and siamang in the area supported this. His investigations suggested that the total population over seven miles of the territory in question was 480, and if one in every ten people used the railway once a week – a very high proportion – they "would contribute a passenger traffic of seven a day or, say, two in each train" – which was hardly the way to run a railroad. A geologist was brought into the fray and he reported on the existence of a stratum of "fine blue plastic sea clay" near Telok Anson and below that of "fine blue-grey granite sand", and below that again of "brown soft clay with pieces of wood" and then of more sand and clay in which, finally and very deeply, one could probably embed three deep-water piers for the proposed railhead.

What with Moss urging the necessity for "more cast-iron work" on the bridges, and the growing number of surveys, traces and underwater explorations carried out, the costs of the project spiralled alarmingly. Swettenham began to wonder about the danger of over-building railways, for it had to be remembered, he cautioned, that rail could not compete in price with the "bullock-buses" that ran along the main roads in Perak, and which carried passengers a very long way for just ten cents because "bullocks cost comparatively little to buy and very little to keep; the carts are rough and inexpensive; harness nil and as the drivers are usually also the owners, a very small sum will support them".

Where roads were not viable propositions, the debate over ways and means split into "the wheels versus the keels" men – the latter arguing that trains should only take over from the points where ships or river-boats could go no further. The Governor was a "keel man" – "short wheel transit and long keel transit will always be cheaper than the reverse", he insisted. And, "natives to whom time means little and money much will calculate the advantages to a nicety and act accordingly."

When Swettenham left the Selangor Residency, discussion over the project, first mooted four years earlier, was still going on and not a sleeper had been laid. Maxwell took it upon himself to investigate certain transactions in the neighbourhood of Klang and Telok Anson in which Moss had bought up land which, he must have known, was likely to be wanted for future wharf development. There was a commission of inquiry, with Maxwell as its President; Moss was dismissed; unspoken doubts were again cast on Swettenham's judgment; someone at the Colonial Office noted irritably on the margin of a dispatch about the scandal, "What ever Mr Maxwell says acts like a red rag with a bull in the case of Mr Swettenham."

From such burdens, barbs and beastly vexations of higher office, the Residents and their senior staffs sought occasional rest and recreation in the hills – the cool limestone outcrops above the steamy, jungled plains that had never been much cherished by the natives. But the British, of different physical constitution, did cherish them. The first Indian-style "hill station" in Malaya was situated on the uplands behind Taiping and by 1889 sufficient accommodation for several officers had been built there. The rule was that only those drawing less than a hundred dollars a month were entitled to a seat at government expense on the box of the omnibus that ran from Taiping. And, cautioned one of many Residential circulars on the subject of government economy, "The expense of a private gharry is not to be incurred instead of the Omnibus except in cases of urgent necessity."

Once arrived, by whatever vehicle, the cool air was such a delicious relief that one felt restored immediately, and how nostalgically like dear home it was when, as one lady visitor wrote, "storm clouds rush up the staircases into the bedrooms and the pillows were wet with damp Scotch mist". On the main elevation, which soon became known as Maxwell Hill, after William Edward, there were three furnished bungalows: "The Bungalow" for married officers, "The Hut" for the bachelors, and "The Tea-Garden Bungalow" which could accommodate three families of unspecified rank. Visitors were requested to replace any damaged articles at their own expense, and please to remember that water-carriers and coolies were not to be employed as house-servants, and that all perishable food must be taken away on departure. The last injunction was probably superfluous for fresh provisions were not easy to come by and those intending to stay a while in the hills had to drive their meat supplies ahead of them up the track – in the shape of a sheep or two and a coolie carrying crates of ducks and hens.

The Superintendent of Maxwell Hill in its early days was Leonard Wray, an experimental botanist generally credited with the introduction of Liberian coffee into the Peninsula. According to the lady visitor, he was "a tall, remarkably slim man who wears no shirt and with a kind of blue cloth coat buttoned up close to the neck with Perak crown buttons, and with a pale, cadaverous-looking face and a crocodile smile". When Hugh Low retired, Wray was one of the few to carry on his enthusiastic faith in the future of rubber and planted some young rubber trees in the grounds of the Taiping Museum. In the cooler gardens on the Hill, Wray experimented with the growing of European vegetables and homely flowers such as begonias and gloxinias sent from Mr Bull of Chelsea – which gladdened the eyes of the officers suffering from debilitating fevers who had come up to recuperate, and their wives who drifted along the leafy lanes collecting wild ferns and orchids.

From the summit of Maxwell Hill one could see as far as the Malacca Straits – where British-built lighthouses now flashed more frequently than the lamps of marauding pirate boats. Between sea and upland, the town of Taiping spread out on the plain; a pleasing sight, wrote Ambrose Rathborne: "Bayonets flashing in the sun as the police go through their evolutions on the parade grounds . . . The green of the acacia trees that line the streets and intermingle with the red-tiled houses of the traders, forming a pleasing contrast of colour. The sombre shingle roofs of the detached dwellings mark the houses in which government officials live, and dwarfed figures in white running to and fro on the green, well-kept cricket ground bear witness that this national game has found a home for itself in this foreign land where inter-station and colony cricket matches are regularly held, and the players, after each innings, discuss its events over cooling drinks in the Club hard by . . ."

For aspiring juniors in the Government Service cricketing skill had become a useful attribute, particularly in Perak where Swetten-ham was the boss. He had always been a very keen sportsman and he felt that the exercise of "conquest and physical mastery on the games field was a fine training ground for healthy-minded English youth". The *Penang Gazette* of 1893, which, in the past, had criticized Swettenham for his "vaulting ambition", reported that there was considerable bitterness "against the system of getting all the best cricketers to go to Taiping . . . Everyone is proud of the Perak Eleven," the editor continued, "but there is no possible excuse for adding gall and wormwood to the majority of young men in the out-stations by making them feel that promotion will depend more on their capabilities in the cricket field than their duties to Government." So strongly did the claims of sport supplant those of work, the paper concluded, that one Mr Thorold had recently left the Service in disgust because he had not been selected to play for the Straits against Ceylon.

Graced with its immaculate cricket ground, its Museum started by Hugh Low, its Rest House opened in the mid-1880s "for the convenience of gentlemen who come to the country with a view to investing in it", Taiping was becoming an attractive social centre for the increasing number of government officials and their families in the area. In 1893 Resident Frank Swettenham performed the opening ceremony of the new Public Gardens, assisted by his wife who turned on the water of a central fountain presented by the Chinese community. The Gardens, Swettenham said in a speech from the bunting-bright dais, would "undoubtedly become a pleasant evening promenade for the people of Taiping" and added that there were plans afoot to make an ornamental lake nearby on the site of some disused tin-workings.

There was also a splendid racecourse, and race days attracted so many visitors that every house in town was filled with them, according to the *Penang Gazette* which described one such occasion: among the crowd were "a great number of ladies, in such pretty and becoming attire and all looking so well that I wonder how such an effect can be produced in these remote parts of the globe," the reporter marvelled. During the interval between the races three buffaloes escaped from the carriage enclosure and, "knocking down some Sikhs who tried to stop their mad career, entered the course and set off at a good pace, but being somewhat entangled together, there was no competition". It was all part of the fun, and so was the Gala Dance held that evening in the Club Reading Room, "which was prettily decorated with flags and the caps and colours of the jockeys". Next day was merry too – a gymkhana with a tent-pegging competition among the Sikh Police and a special animal race, the entrants for which included two dogs, a toad, a small pig and a paddy bird. And the day after the District Officers and their wives, the engineers, doctors and planters mounted their saddle ponies, gharries, bullock-carts and went back to "the jungle" – a little out of pocket probably, but much cheered up.

While all these "civilizing improvements", as the press termed them, were forging ahead in Taiping under Swettenham's direction, Maxwell in Kuala Lumpur was not sitting idly. Indeed, the Selangor capital was getting "improved" and "civilized" even more rapidly and on a more dramatic scale. One hundred and seventy-three acres of Public Gardens with flowering trees and shrubs were firmly established there by 1892 and in that spring Resident Maxwell, "under a particularly scorching sun, performed the ceremony of planting the first tree on the banks of the Sydney Lake, which had been made by damming part of the river". The press, reporting the occasion, added that there had been several complaints from residents recently about the dreadful native habit of using the ornamental waters for unornamental purposes. As one aggrieved correspondent put it, "when one is conducting a lady round the lake of the Public Gardens it is not pleasant to be confronted at every ten yards with dusky nude specimens refreshing themselves after the toil of the day in water about a foot deep". To prevent further embarrassment, the editor suggested that thatch screens should be erected around a designated bathing area in a more remote spot.

By the early 1890s a certain sense of propriety, order, fitness and stability was as firmly implanted in the growing capital as the ornamental trees in the Public Gardens, and the haphazard, smelly, makeshift mining settlement of twenty years earlier was no more. Yap Ah Loy's eldest son lived rather splendidly in a brick villa on the hill; the plank shed that housed the original Club had been replaced by a grander building in the Victorio-Elizabethan manner facing the main *padang*, colloquially called the Spotted Dog – supposedly after the dalmatian belonging to Mrs Syers, wife of the

Chief of Police, that was frequently tied to the verandah posts. The town could boast of an efficient volunteer fire brigade to man an engine drawn by shire horses imported from England; there were three bakeries and three pillar-boxes, in addition to the central Post and Telegraph Office; there was the Penang and Perak Aerated Water Factory, its every bottle emblazoned with a testimonial from Sir Hugh Low to the effect that it contained the most superior soda water manufactured in the Straits Settlements. In the newly built, sanitary-inspected food market one could buy such imported delicacies as Australian tinned butter, anchovies and Lea & Perrins sauce, as well as a great variety of local produce – from ducks to durians, from coconut-fibre brooms to buffalo tongues.

Time was properly marked by the firing of a gun from the Police Fort on Bluff Road at 5 a.m., noon and 9 p.m. curfew. On the appointed days and seasons Resident Maxwell came down from his Residency on the hill, where the British flag flew, his piercing eye sweeping the musters of his men – on the parade ground, in offices, in church – to note any absentees; and Mrs Maxwell would be At Home twice a month to callers. Trains, carrying kerosene, beer, salt fish, pig-iron, jungle-posts and "Manchester Goods" as well as passengers, puffed regularly in and out of the station, which, wrote a lady resident of the period, was "quite like a pretty country one with bungalows for most of the railway people nearby". Sometimes, in the late afternoons when the sun was mellowing from bright white to gold, Captain Syers went out with dog and gun to shoot snipe in the swamp at the far end of the *padang*, and there might be an early evening concert by the police band in the park.

High points of the seasonal social calendar – the Queen's Birthday, St George's Day, New Year – were formally marked by Residency Receptions. At one such, held in the summer of 1893, the press noted that "Lady Mitchell wore a dress of rich black moiré trimmed with old lace; Mrs Treacher was charmingly attired in a gown of pale blue satin with corsage and trimming of black jewelled net; Mrs Spooner's tall figure bore with much grace a plum-coloured velvet trimmed with lovely old lace; while

Mrs Stafford's gown of pale pink satin and Mrs Maynard's dress of pink brocade were much admired".

For less formal occasions, when someone ordinary had a birthday or just felt like celebrating, an evening putting match on the golf course might be got up, followed by a moonlit picnic supper at the ninth hole. Thus reclining near the clubhouse, in a rattan chair with a glass of champagne under the swimming stars, one might readily imagine that the "jungle" had been entirely banished from the land and that all the "natives" had been conveniently Europeanized – like the few young swells one saw in their carriages at the races, sporting dark trousers, stiff wing collars, smoking caps and tinted spectacles.

But the take-over was by no means complete. Crocodiles sometimes swam up-river to forage among the fish-guts and offal from the market stalls; gibbons hooted from the trees behind the rich Chinese villas in the suburbs; in one of the houses along the Batu Road twenty goats, two cows and a sheep were found penned on the verandah, "and this state of things, in one of the principal streets of the town, can hardly be called a credit to our Municipality", the local paper commented. Even less creditable was the alarming experience of a guest at the Rest House who, when sitting in his darkened bedroom one evening, "heard a noise behind him, called out 'Boy', and a large black cobra jumped at him".

The jungle still waited and, in the wood and thatch *kampongs*, the easy languid rhythms of planting and gathering still went on, not many miles from the clubhouse verandah. One of the main changes in tempo was being caused by the spread of plantation agriculture into the rural areas. By the end of 1893 there were nineteen European-owned estates totalling some 12,300 acres in Selangor, nearly all around Kuala Lumpur and Klang and nearly all concentrating on the cultivation of Liberian coffee. For the growing of coffee, which had been a disaster only a few years before, was enjoying a short-lived boom, owing to the rise in world prices and the fact that Tamil labourers from South India were now allowed in as immigrants.

Tamils, according to Rathborne, were not nearly so "physically or constitutionally strong as the Chinese, and suffered much more from the climate, becoming thin and fever-stricken". But they were "amenable and easily managed" if treated fairly, and would work for lower wages, which made them an attractive proposition to planters and conveniently kept them in a more humble socio-economic position than the thrusting Chinese, whose numbers had also increased. In the view of Frank Swettenham, who had first seen the under-populated wastes of the Native States twenty years before, this continuing influx of foreign labour must be entirely good for the country. Much of the credit for its success was, he felt, due to government officers who encouraged the immigrants and, with a benevolent paternalism worthy of a good squire in the old country, "nursed them in every possible way, made things pleasant for them, knew them all, took an interest in them, praising their cottages and their gardens, giving them the energy they often lacked and even imbuing them with a spirit of rivalry which led to the building of villages, the planting of orchards, the cultivation of profitable produce and so to a pride in their surroundings which amounted to the gift of a new sense".

William Maxwell, on the other hand, was never an unequivocal supporter of the planting community because he alleged that some planters bought up land and then speculated with it. Also, he had a commitment to the traditional unit of the small Malay village which, he realized, would be drastically changed by the spread of large-scale plantation agriculture and that this, in turn, would have an impact on rural custom and culture. His views on this were shared by Hugh Clifford, whose deep emotional response to the beautiful serenities of the Malay countryside had not lessened with the years. After his prolonged sick leave, Clifford had returned to Pahang in 1890 and was Acting Resident there for various periods during the next five years.

In Pahang the times were still troublous, for there was considerable opposition to the new arrangements for the collection of revenue and land-rents, and armed groups led by war-like chiefs openly rebelled against the imposition of British authority. A Sikh force from Perak was sent in to quell the disturbances and Clifford therefore found himself involved in the task of leading his men into action against the natives and punishing the "rebels". It was an unfortunate role for him personally, as his views about the intrinsic rightness of the British presence in the country remained ambivalent and contradictory. His conviction that only relentless and rapid suppression would bring "the wished-for peace" to everyone kept him going, but not very happily. Of a fictional Political Agent in an identical situation, he wrote that "those gainst whom he fought were his own people, among whom he had lived for years, and he suffers with them in spirit, groaning over the necessity that drives him to persecute them. It is an impossible frame of mind and one that makes his days bitter to him."

In other respects life in Pahang was rather more pleasant than it had been earlier. His job and his status in the community were more clearly defined and he spent much time in the usual governmental pursuit of travelling around and writing reports on his observations. And that was the best part of the job, for the empty wilds held a life-long fascination for him, their freedoms and hardships providing constant challenge to his body and spirit. He never became a desk-man at heart, but he did now have an office in which to write and receive the numerous people who came to him with their grievances and problems. There were a few more other foreigners about too – mining engineers, hopeful planters, junior officials – so that the isolation from his own kind was less severe: "Played lawn tennis with Smyth and won" runs an uncharacteristic entry in his 1893 journal, the same year that he made a trip to the Siamese-held state of Trengannu with Sir Cecil Smith, the new Governor of the Straits Settlements.

The trouble though was that Pahang refused to live up to the optimistic forecasts of its potential prosperity which had been made by Sir Frederick Weld – and echoed by Swettenham and Clifford – when the British had first infiltrated there. The government in Singapore was forced to lend Pahang large sums for development and a number of companies based in Europe bought up land for mining – but Pahang remained poor, under-populated, unwieldy and "unregenerate", still, in the British mind, the haunt of wild beasts and primitive savages. It was an impression reinforced by one British traveller who, after venturing into those

great deal of harm because "there was no one in Singapore who had knowledge enough to criticize the actions of the Residents successfully". Knowledge had to be bang up to date to be of any use, for, "in twelve months a considerable mining town would spring up in the midst of what had been virgin forest and the Residents would write to Singapore of roads and places never before heard of and not to be found on any map". Crucial to the success of any Federation scheme therefore, Swettenham argued, was the creation of a new post of a chief executive officer who would be entitled Resident General and act as the main channel of communication and information between the government in Singapore and the Residents of the various states, over whom he would have authority. Knowing the personality of Frank Athelstane Swettenham, it is not difficult to guess whom F.A.S. had in mind as the first occupant of that elevated position.

For a time, Swettenham's ambitions were checked by the retirement of Sir Cecil Smith, who had been his supporter, and the subsequent appointment as Governor of Sir Charles Mitchell, who came from Natal and admitted to an almost total ignorance of Malayan affairs. He was a cautious, heavy, dry man; Swettenham noted that when Mitchell visited Kuala Kangsa soon after taking up office and was greeted with the usual official warmth, "he acknowledged that attention with the remark, 'I am glad you have given me such a cordial welcome, for I am sure you will not repeat it when I leave'." He also informed Swettenham that he possessed "an economic soul – a description he reiterated whenever an extensive work was suggested".

However, Charles Lucas, Swettenham's friend at court, continued to do his bit by setting out, in a number of well-reasoned memoranda, the various advantages of a centralized administration, clarifying the limits of Residential and Resident General's authority and suggesting ways in which at least the nominal autonomy and character of the separate States could be preserved. Swettenham, for his part, could point to the ever-increasing success of his administration in Perak. It was a success which he judged primarily in purely economic terms, as evidenced in his proud annual report of 1894 where he claimed that "the wealthiest

Malays in the Peninsula are Perak Malays. It is for them that the richest silks of Trengannu and Batu Bara are woven, it is they who vie with each other in the building of expensive houses and the possession of horses and carriages, while many of them own residences in the Sacred City of Mecca."

Perak, it seemed, had out-distanced Selangor in the progress-to-prosperity stakes, which made Swettenham jubilant, even though his hated rival, Maxwell, was no longer the Selangor Resident, because he had been transferred back to Singapore as the Colonial Secretary. Maxwell, naturally, was against the kind of Federation scheme proposed by Swettenham and his supporters, and so too was Maxwell's Colonial Office chum, Edward Fairfield, who doubted Swettenham's capacity for the senior post: "He is a headstrong man, and I think the new office would turn his head and we should find him a trouble," he minuted. But the tide was running against them – as Maxwell undoubtedly realized in the summer of 1894 when Fairfield wrote him a gently exploratory letter about his future ambitions. Maxwell replied to the effect that he would indeed consider possibilities of postings to other colonies: "There is such a thing as knowing too much about things and people," he told Fairfield, and, in consequence, he would not be "very sorry" to leave the Straits Settlements.

Several months later Sir Charles Mitchell was finally persuaded to favour federation of the kind proposed, officially, by Sir Charles Lucas in the Colonial Office; Fairfield, accepting defeat, remarked that he assumed "all the numerous advocates of the measure on the spot will take occasion to increase their own salaries". On 6th June 1895 Mitchell received definite instructions by telegram from the Secretary of State to go ahead with the plan, providing the Malay rulers agreed. Swettenham took over from that point and everything suddenly moved very fast. After all, federation was really a simple little arrangement that need not incommode anyone, because, Swettenham wrote, it "disturbs no existing arrangements, breaks no promises, doesn't alter the status of the Malay rulers..." And so, "having discussed the matter very thoroughly with the Governor and my fellow Residents, I prepared a detailed scheme of reorganization and drafted short agreements which, by the

Governor's instructions, I took to each of the four Rulers and to five chiefs of minor States in Negri Sembilan, and obtained the signatures of all the Malays concerned. The document is dated July, 1895, and when completed I was appointed to the post of Resident General and began at once to put the scheme into operation."

10

"The reality of 'Federation'"

So, in 1896, the rather dashing, very astute and confident forty-five-year-old Frank Swettenham was formally installed as Resident General with, as he himself describes it, "General control over the Residents – subject to the instructions of the Governor", whose yet-superior position was emphasized by adding to *his* title that of "High Commissioner for the Federated Malay States". The year before, Swettenham's long-standing rival, William Maxwell, taking the hint from the Colonial Office, asked for and was appointed to the Governorship of the Gold Coast instead. He applied himself energetically to the affairs of the new colony and was beginning to prove that he could be an equally able "Africa man" when he was felled by blackwater fever and died after only two years in office.

Ultimately overshadowed and defeated by Swettenham, the value of Maxwell's work in the organization and translation of the Malay legal codes and his efforts to harmonize Asian custom and English law were long underrated. Possessed of an incisive and agile intelligence, great determination and integrity, he yet lacked the affability, the sheer style which made Swettenham popular with most of his colleagues and subordinates. The Peninsula was not really big enough to hold both of them comfortably, and eventually Swettenham won the day.

The creation of the Resident General's post, though not, in theory, supposed to diminish further the importance and authority of the Malay rulers of the separate States, did just that in practice. The very existence of an increasingly comprehensive and centralized bureaucracy which was administered "for and on behalf of the Rulers" meant that each Sultanate had less individual identity. Policies were framed in relation to the needs of the Protected States as a whole, and the Sultans became little more than their official rubber-stampers – which meant that the very word "Federation" was a misnomer. In compensation, the rulers were certainly accorded more wealth and dignity than formerly – which satisfied some more than others.

Federation also meant the beginning of the end of the State Councils, which no longer had control over State finances and no say in the recruitment of people into the administration. Nor were the members of the Councils in such direct contact with the principal decision-makers, for the Residents themselves had also lost much of their former autonomous, if localized, power, and were now civil servants under the Resident General's direction. However, as an historian has said, "The Rulers and his chiefs still looked upon the Resident as 'their man' who would support them against any other Resident or, if need arose, make a fight with them against the Resident General. Although most of the power had been taken out of the hands of the Residents, it was psychologically expedient to preserve the institution of Resident-ship, for, in the Residential system, form was more important than content." And so the Residential office remained an uneasy compromise, as it had always been – and now something of an anachronism within the modern governmental framework that Swettenham was busy building.

At his headquarters in Kuala Lumpur an increasing number of specialist departments proliferated, each under a Federal Head – for Railways, Post and Telegraph, Surveys, Mines – all the familiar names, but writ very much larger. And there were new names as well: a Legal Adviser, a Judicial Commissioner, a Conservator of Forests, a Superintendent of Indian Immigrants, an Accountant General and Auditor, a Chief Inspector of Schools . . . each and all of them taking instructions from and reporting back to Swettenham. To house all these officials a new government secretariat was built in the town in 1897; it was of warm pink brick cut with Moorish-style arches, with a 130-foot-high onion-domed clock tower, embellished with sprightly minarets and it was considered an adventurous example of "Arabesque Renaissance" or "Saracenic Moslem"!

Whatever the uneasy equilibrium of authority between the Federal Heads in the new Secretariat and the Residents in their States, they had all been recruited from similar ranks. The ideal cadets for the Malay Civil Service, created in 1896 as a unified administrative corps for the Protected States as a whole, were, in the words of the Governor, "young men of good physique and energetic and fearless disposition, of moderate attainments and, if possible, well brought up". Aspirants for the M.C.S. had to pass examinations similar to those for the other colonial services and those who qualified were informed that, having elected to live in a tropical climate, they must "make up their minds to conform from the first to the cardinal rules for the preservation of their health" – as outlined in the Government's Year Book. The positive injunctions included going to bed and getting up early and always wearing flannel next to the skin; the negatives were never to drink to excess, go out between 8 a.m. and 4.30 p.m. without wearing a topee, or drink from a roadside stream.

New arrivals were also warned that life was expensive in the Malay States and that it was not safe for the newcomer "to cut his estimate of annual expenses down to any lower figure than one which exceeds by half what he has found requisite in England". This estimate was appropriate for "bachelor gentlemen of education and refinement" to live "with any approach to comfort", though "emigrants of the artisan class" might be able to manage on rather less. However, very few openings for "artisans" existed; for practically all government posts two qualifications were essential: a white face and a public-school education.

Of course, Swettenham and his colleagues agreed that Malays must be given every encouragement to join the Service also and take more responsibility for government – but it just did not seem to happen. After Federation, as before it, Malays were employed as *penghulus* and policemen, and a few were magistrates. Even young Malays of considerable ability were reluctant to join the government ranks, partly because they had nearly all received a vernacular education which neither tempted nor qualified them for work in a Western-style bureaucracy. Swettenham's view was that a few Malays would be capable of this, providing they were exposed to a sufficient degree of sound moral European training. And he cited three examples of rajas who proved really quite "earnest, capable and energetic", even without "the experience of an English school". And, he continued, "A Far Eastern race which can produce men like these men who developed principles as high as those which guide the best Europeans and strive to live up to them, is not to be despised or dismissed as useless."

Nevertheless, Swettenham was uneasily aware that, in the interests of centralization and economic efficiency, ever greater distances were being created between the administrators and the native population. It was an attempt to bridge these and, Swettenham wrote, "bring home to the Malay Rulers in the most striking manner possible the reality of 'Federation'" that a Conference, bringing together the Sultans, members of the State Councils and senior British officials, was held at Kuala Kangsa in July 1897, at the grand palace of Sultan Idris. "Such a meeting," Swettenham claimed, "had never been known in the history of Malaya, where each Ruler was too much on his dignity or too unfriendly to think of visiting a neighbour." But to this they all came – even the proud, autocratic Sultan of Pahang, even the seemingly indestructible Sultan of Selangor, Abdul Samad, who was then ninety-three years old and still living at Langat.

After the High Commissioner, up from Singapore, had opened the proceedings, the first business of the day was the sending of a telegram from the assembled Sultans to Queen Victoria, offering Her Majesty, "Respectful and cordial congratulations on a reign of unexampled length and unequalled progress", and with prayers for "Your Majesty's long life and the continuance of that protection which has already brought such prosperity to Malaya". Not a great deal else was accomplished in terms of policy-making, though a Land Code for all the States was unanimously adopted. There was much feasting and entertainment – jungle picnics, firework-displays, fishing expeditions, water sports, amateur theatricals – and everyone apparently enjoyed it. One old Pahang chief reputedly remarked to Hugh Clifford afterwards that, "until we visited Perak, we were like unto the frog beneath a coconut shell, not dreaming there were other worlds than ours"; the Resident of Negri Sembilan said that the chiefs of that State "have been raised to a concept of good government which they had not previously contemplated" by attending the Conference. Swettenham too was full of enthusiasm and told the Colonial Office that it was difficult "to estimate now the present and prospective value of this unprecedented gathering".

Most of the ruling Malays, like the ruling British, undoubtedly enjoyed the pomp and circumstance of such formal occasions which created a feeling of mutual trust and goodwill. As a modern historian, commenting on the Conference's lack of any legislative enactments, remarked, "In the art of indirect rule, the setting of the stage is perhaps more important than the actual performance of the players and this fact an astute administrator like Swettenham, who had a thorough knowledge of Malay psychology, must have grasped and exploited fully." Certainly Swettenham could and did justly claim that the Conference was very tangible and definite evidence that, under British rule, the country was much less riven by warring factions than in his early days when "every Malay had as many weapons as he could carry; say, two daggers in his belt, two spears in his hand, a gun over his shoulder and a long sword under his arm. Now the men carry umbrellas and the boys slates and books . . ."

Within this tidy and peaceful order of things, the Resident whose general life-style could still most closely approximate to the earlier Residential ideal was the office-holder in Pahang, the State which remained largely cut-off from the main administrative stream and was several decades behind the west coast in terms of economic development and modernization. Pahang was still Hugh Clifford's beat. He was finally made Resident there in 1896, the year in which he married and took his young wife, formerly Mary Beckett, to live in the Pahang Residency, where his first two children were born. By this time Clifford was in his thirties and, while still a strong advocate of Progress For Pahang, his growing maturity brought a growing awareness that the changes progress wrought were not always for the good.

There are wistful passages in his stories about the quiet delights of slow-boat river travel compared to the noise and rush of trains, and the fact that the picturesque indigenous elephants were of much less use on the new metalled-surface roads. In his earlier period of office, when Pahang was without any form of inter-State communication, Clifford longed for it; now that there was a telegraph, a regular, if fairly perilous, boat service and talk of a connecting railway, he paradoxically mourned the passing of the total and pristine isolation of the so-recent past. The advance of "progress" was a mixed blessing for the Malays also he felt, and those of the west coast were already becoming "sadly dull, limp and civilized" compared to their former "truculent and untamed state". Whereas, in the unspoiled vastnesses of the east, "the lover of things as they are and ought not to be, may find a dwelling among an unregenerate and more or less uncivilized people whose customs are still unsullied by European vulgarity".

And yet the absolutes could not be denied; distinctions must still be made between what "ought" and "ought not" to be; he still believed that, flawed and ambivalent as they were, the imperial imperatives of civilization and progress had to be upheld and furthered. In the preface of his collection of stories, *In Court and Kampong*, published in 1897, he wrote, "One may perhaps feel some measure of sentimental sorrow that the natural should here, as elsewhere, be replaced by the artificial . . . But no one who has seen the horrors of native rule and the misery to which people living under it are often reduced, can find room to doubt that, its many drawbacks not withstanding, the only salvation for the Malays lies in the increase of British influence in the Peninsula." Nevertheless and secretly, he *did* still find room for doubt and, in the long warm watches of the Pahang night, beset, as always by insomnia, he wondered if there were not other ways of Westernizing this backward East? And he pondered the creation of some sort of idyllic and innocuous governing system which would protect the people from the worst excesses and harshness of the feudal past, bring them some prosperity and yet not totally destroy their traditional rural life.

Waking dreams only, prophetic of many twentieth-century

dilemmas; visions that were not, in any case, shared by those with the most authority, who dealt in certainties. By 1899, Swettenham wrote, the people of the Peninsula were truly grateful for British intervention and were "freer, healthier, wealthier, more independent, more enlightened – happier by far than in the days of Malay rule". Certain criteria bore this out, for the natives of Pahang were considerably poorer, less well nourished and with fewer educational opportunities than those of the States which had been under British protection for twenty years. Clifford, pushing strongly for the expansion of Pahang's educational system and the improvement of its agricultural productivity, reported that, in bad years, its rice yields were insufficient for the population's needs. This, he said, was because cultivators took little care to protect their crops from the depredations of wild pigs, mice or a large and greedy species of jungle bat and still relied on extravagant short-term methods of "slash and burn" cultivation – which meant that "acres of valuable timber were burned each year for the sake of a few extra sacks of rice". But, unfortunately, the Pahangese "dislike innovation of any kind and are slow to adopt improved agricultural implements or modes of agriculture which differ from those employed by their fathers before them".

Agriculturists, in general a fairly conservative breed, frequently prefer their fathers' methods of cultivation; but the European planters in the Peninsula had to adapt quickly to new circumstances in order to survive. The coffee boom of the early 1890s was already past its peak by 1896 due to increased competition from Brazil, and by 1900 many of the smaller planters of Liberian coffee faced bankruptcy. It was at last time for the rubber enthusiasts to come into their own and in 1898 Swettenham, regaining his earlier interest in the crop's potential, introduced regulations to encourage rubber cultivation. Within five years most of the European-owned coffee estates on the west coast were interplanted with rubber, and even Chinese farmers, who had always eschewed rubber because of its long maturation period, began to plant some trees between their tapioca, coconuts and gambier. Improvements to road and rail communications were undertaken to facilitate the transport of latex to the ports, and the outlook for the Peninsula as a whole was again suddenly rosy.

With everything thus going for him it was hardly surprising that, in 1901, Swettenham scaled the very pinnacle of his career – when he succeeded Sir Charles Mitchell as Governor of the Straits Settlements and High Commissioner of the Federated Malay States. It was a measure of his dynamic and compelling personality that the centre of direction and control then shifted with him from Kuala Lumpur to Singapore – for the new Resident General, Sir William Treacher (who had, incidentally, once served in dismal Labuan with Hugh Low) was conscientious and retiring, willing to defer to Swettenham, as he had in the past. And Swettenham, the born autocrat, kept a firm hand on affairs in both the Protected States and Singapore – it meant double the work, but he had never been afraid of that.

Socially too Swettenham's horizons expanded, for Singapore, unlike Kuala Lumpur, was on the fashionable Eastern globe-trotting circuit, and all the best people naturally stayed at Government House. The Duke and Duchess of Cornwall with a royal entourage of nineteen arrived in the sumptuous yacht *Ophir* and Sultan Idris of Perak came to town for the occasion, bringing his mounted Sikh escort and his State carriage – drawn by four horses with English postilions – to carry the royal pair around on their junketings. Gertrude Bell also turned up unexpectedly, "an exhilarating companion," Swettenham noted, "whose own gifts brought out the best in others"; and several ageing European military leaders, some deaf, some a trifle lame and all apparently very jolly, called in on their way to or from China, where they had been engaged in the relief of the besieged embassies in Peking and the mopping-up operations that followed the Boxer Rebellion.

In the summer of 1903 a second Conference of Malay chiefs was held – this time in Kuala Lumpur. It was "equally successful", according to Swettenham, and was also noteworthy because the rulers of the western states were all conveyed thither by train for the first time. Sultan Idris made a remarkable closing speech in which he gave a graphic account "of the benefits which had been conferred on the country and the people by the adoption of British methods of administration . . . His Highness laid special stress on the fact that he and his people had given their confidence and lasting friendship to those Residents who came with the evident wish to secure them."

However, Swettenham omits to record that Idris – the heir apparent tutored into acquiescence by Hugh Low in his youth, but now come to a deeper personal understanding of all the issues involved – also protested against the prevailing trend towards centralization, reminding his listeners that the original Engagement of Pangkor had provided for a number of Residents who would advise the rulers of each state on a close, individual basis, not for the issuing of directives from the remote head of a European-dominated bureaucracy. Sultan Idris was the most respected and authoritative of the Malay rulers and usually acted as their spokesman, and it is likely that the dissatisfaction he mildly expressed was shared among them. But that Swettenham makes no mention of this in his book is typical for, from the days of his earliest reports – written late at night by candlelight in his stockade on the Langat swamp – he always contrived to put on record mainly those things that would add lustre to the image of Frank Athelstane Swettenham, as tenacious and successful diplomat, as resourceful and courageous leader of men, as the top expert on any local scene. He was all that; he was also, one suspects, not over-scrupulous in all his dealings; he could be arrogant, high-handed and snobbish; he could be ruthless. And, in spite of the amount he wrote about himself and the country where he spent the most constructive years of his life, there is something devious about him.

As there was over the matter of his resignation. For, given the prestige and authority of his position as Governor and High Commissioner, it is difficult to guess why, after serving only half his term, he decided to retire at the end of 1903. Certainly he had had, as he wrote, "a rather strenuous service of over thirty years in an enervating climate", and he said he wanted to relinquish the post before he became a burden to the country. There was no immediate fear of that, for he was a very capable man in his early fifties with many years ahead of him. Probably the principal reason for his decision was financial. Swettenham had always thought a great deal about money – it is clear from his earliest accounts which carefully record the price of every bag of rice and tips for every boatman. Despite holding the highest paid post in the Straits Settlements he was not really a wealthy man, though he liked a lot of expensive sports and entertained lavishly; as a civil servant however, he could not seize the opportunities of making profitable investments in the tin, rubber and other industries about which he was highly knowledgeable. There may well have been the contributory personal factor of his very unsatisfactory marriage to Constance Holmes, the daughter of a Harrow schoolmaster, whom he had married in 1878 and eventually divorced after sixty years of wedlock on the grounds that she had long been "of unsound mind". Such a partner must have been a cause of strain and worry in the active high-level social life of Singapore.

Swettenham himself is unusually reticent on the subject of his retirement. He simply writes that, when he left Singapore in October 1903, there was a large party held in his honour at Government House where he "had the pleasure of hearing and saying those last words which remain as a precious memory of good friendship and mutual regard. Then there was a parting on the wharf at Tanjong Pagar, and with Captain Barry and G. A. V. Bosanquet – my A.D.C. and private secretary – who went with me – we watched from the deck the gradually disappearing crowd of friends as the Messageries steamer pushed her way through the narrows of the winding passage to the open sea; that was farewell to Malaya."

11

Frailties and Foibles

There is a picture of Sir Frank Swettenham, G.C.M.G., C.H., as
frontispiece to his autobiographical book *Footprints in Malaya*. He
is wearing all the insignia appropriate to his last public appointment: the collar and wrists of his uniform are stiff with embroi-
dered gold; across his chest are displayed so many medals and
chains of office that, had he walked, he must have jingled a little.
But he sits, his cold eyes staring confidently into the distance – the
imperturbable and incorruptible ruler of natives, an Empire
builder, a man of purpose and achievement, stern, square-jawed,
middle-aged.

He published that book in 1941 when he was ninety years old
and still had five years to live. I have always found it hard to
believe that I was therefore twelve years old when he died and
could actually have met him – albeit in a gymslip and with nothing
whatsoever, at that time, that I could possibly have said to him.
Now, of course, there is so much I would want to know about
what those Residents were really like when they were not posing
for official frontispiece pictures or writing official dispatches to the
Governor of the Straits Settlements or the Colonial Office. What
about the interstices, the frailties and foibles which, in Victorian
times particularly, it was seldom thought appropriate to put on
record?

I should like to know, for a start, what the young cadet Frank
was thinking that evening when he stood over the grave of James
Woodford Wheeler Birch on the swampy island of Bandar Bharu
and read the time-honoured last service and heard the funeral guns
firing their respects to the dead. Certainly he himself had just had a

very close call, and there is an entry in a Blue Book for 9th November 1875 written by Captain Tristram Speedy informing the Singapore Governor of the probable murder of Swettenham and Lieutenant Abbott, the lucky snipe-shooter, and saying that men had been dispatched "to obtain, if possible, the remains of these unfortunate officers".

Swettenham, who had more than a flash of the swashbuckler himself, was never one of Speedy's many detractors and he includes a photograph of the Captain in full Abyssinian fig in two of his books. Swettenham says that when he first met Speedy and his wife they were in charge of the son of King Theodore of Abyssinia, who was later taken from them and sent to an English public school "where he pined, sickened and died". Speedy had apparently been most upset by this and vowed never to shave again till some sort of reparation was made for the boy's death, which was why he sported such a very lengthy beard – and, when Swettenham met the six-feet-six-inch-tall Captain again in Larut in 1874, "he was decidedly noticeable".

The re-encounter took place, Swettenham explains, when he and William Pickering – a "China expert" – were sent to ensure that the promises made at Pangkor by the Chinese headmen to restore peace in the turbulent Larut district were actually being carried out. The cross-country trek by elephant to Assistant Resident Speedy's headquarters was apparently one of the most ghastly of all the journeys that the much-travelled Swettenham ever made. There were four of them aboard the elephant: Swettenham, Pickering, one Captain Dunlop and a "Chinese colleague" – who, like most foreigners other than royalty, remains unnamed in British annals.

They set off, he and Pickering seated precariously on some wet grass in the open panier facing the animal's tail. The track, "where it was not an unbroken stretch of water, was a succession of holes at least two feet deep and full of water" – which had been made by other elephants' earlier ploddings. "After an hour's progress it became darker than I have ever known it before, and darkness in dense jungle feels at least doubly dark. We could no more see our own hands than if they had been in the next State, so we were obliged to abandon ourselves entirely to the sagacity of the elephant." It began to rain in tropical bucketfuls; they had no waterproofs and any umbrella "would have been torn to pieces by the branches we could not even see". In order to give a faint guiding clue to their wretched servants who were struggling along on foot through the prickly mires behind, in great fear of being lost or eaten by tigers, Swettenham and Pickering kept puffing cigars and lighting matches and shouting encouragement in their general direction.

"We crossed three considerable rivers in flood," Swettenham continues. "We saw nothing, but we felt the elephant make preparations as though to stand on his head; then he evidently slid down a steep bank; we heard him ploughing through the water and held on for our lives as he crawled up the opposite bank." At midnight, wet through, muddy and exhausted, they reached Captain Speedy's bungalow, where "we borrowed some sacks as night clothes, wrapped ourselves in old tents and were soon fast asleep". The next day, incidentally, Speedy appeared to be quite "green with envy" at the twin accomplishments of William Pickering, which were to speak fluent Chinese and to play the bagpipes. According to Swettenham, it was to mitigate this envy that Speedy procured those bagpipes from Penang and "went marching up and down and blowing with great energy", though the sounds he emitted "were merely discordant noises". Anyway, it was undoubtedly early experiences such as that night's ride which made Swettenham such a convinced rail-and-roads-for-progress man, and which he undoubtedly·quoted at those latter-day romantics like Hugh Clifford when they waxed nostalgic for the good old days on the elephant's back.

Just before he retired, Swettenham had the satisfaction of seeing motor-cars running over metalled-surface roads where elephants had once trod – though, in the early 1900s, such vehicles were still very much a novelty and mostly owned by the Malay royalty. Sultan Idris of Perak owned one of the first and motored in some style. Two footmen with yellow flags stood on the vehicle's wide splashboards to wave bullock-carts, rickshaws and even the occasional elephant from its path. In the car's wake a Sikh bodyguard in royal scarlet, "toiled in vain to keep up with the march of progress, spurring their Australian chargers so that they might, if possible, be at the Palace when His Highness alighted from that inconsiderate carriage with the devil in its iron belly".

The man who wrote that was Richard Winstedt, a Malay scholar, later to be famous, who went to Perak as a Malay Civil Service cadet in 1902 and, after only one year, was appointed an Assistant Inspector of Schools. For, as he wrote, those were still "the happy-go-lucky days when a knowledge of irregular verbs and an aptitude for games were considered adequate equipment for a schoolmaster". A few months later, he continues, "I was appointed to act as Chief to myself, namely Inspector of Schools in addition: there were no superfluous government officers before the advent of Para rubber, and Education did not produce revenue". It was in this capacity that Winstedt was posted to Kuala Kangsa – where, one day, he watched Sultan Idris drive up to the Palace to attend a formal luncheon.

While waiting for the dignitaries to arrange themselves, Winstedt recalls that he chatted to a "Raja with a prognathous jaw and a boxer's nose" who was attired in "neat European tweeds, the only touch of the Orient about him being a neat pork-pie cap". Winstedt, a newcomer just learning Malay, struggled to speak to him in that tongue, but the Raja replied in good English: "Yes, His Highness is coming in his new motor-car. We Malays call it a devil carriage . . . In Java the Susuhunan had a lot of trouble with the body of his car as he may not sit lower than the chauffeur. We Malays have a lot of foolish old customs."

Winstedt did not discover till later that the tweedy Raja was none other than the "feckless and irresponsible" ex-Sultan Abdullah who, as he says, "had himself thirty years before conducted a very foolish old ceremony, the most famous in the annals of Perak". He was referring to the long-ago occasion when Abdullah had tried raising the spirits to see if they would help him rid his State of its first bossy and tactless Resident – J. W. W. Birch. According to Winstedt, who made a study of the original Malay sources, the young Abdullah gathered together for the seance his favoured chiefs, court women with incense and tambourines, and the State Magician who was "beating a drum with gnarled brown fingers and chanting an invocation". Three times, according to witnesses, the spirits entered the body of Sultan Abdullah, who sat on a palm mat with a yellow silk scarf over his head, and three times, "They promised to help the royal medium against the man with light eyes . . . Then the State Magician made a figure of the Resident out of flour, which he and the Sultan stabbed several times. The State Magician also struck the mannikin with a fan, until there flew out of it a butterfly soul which he hit with a knife, drawing blood."

The blood flowed all right, and the body of Birch, duly stabbed, floated down the Perak River shortly after that seance; but the spirits were not very good at follow-through – as Abdullah must have felt when, the next year, he was sentenced by the British to exile in the Seychelles. During his long exile Abdullah learned to wear European dress nattily and talk fluent English, ride in a "devil carriage" and call it a motor-car, and now he was back, standing next to a young M.C.S. cadet and chatting about his favourite subjects which, Winstedt says, were still "ceremonies, ladies and dress", till Sultan Idris' car drew up.

The Sultan emerged, having tactfully allowed his mounted Sikh bodyguard time to line up, and was ushered up the steps of the Palace "by five pages dressed in white duck uniforms with black velvet caps slashed with yellow and white silk". The tiffin which followed lived long in the annals of the Malay Civil Service, Winstedt recalled, because it was specially named after "the twin vessels promoted to honour on the sideboard", which brought a blush to the cheeks of the Perak Resident's wife, and were, presumably, chamber pots. After the lengthy meal, which was the best Malay cuisine served in full-blown Western style and washed down with beer and champagne for the foreign guests, there was a further ceremony at which a young member of the nobility was installed by the Sultan as a "Sri Maharaja". In the course of the installation, Sultan Idris "moistened the youth's forehead with magic water from a bowl at his feet, tucked a bunch of *eylow chempaka* blossoms under the side of his head-kerchief and sprinkled him with rice". At its close, "A Raja who signed himself

'Pot Lorrit' recited a court ode comparing the British Resident with a red hibiscus out of a garden of paradise". The occasion was vibrant with echoes of the past, for the name of the newly-installed Maharaja was Lela. At the end of the day those of sufficiently high rank got into their cars and were driven away; Winstedt went on with his school-inspecting; the ex-Sultan Abdullah returned to the little house in the grounds of Idris' Palace that he had been allotted. "Before that prognathous jaw fell for ever," Winstedt concludes, "he became almost blind and his constant cry was, 'If only I could have foreseen, if I could only have foreseen'."

Similar agonies of hindsight probably afflicted some of those European planters who, having failed with coffee and spurned the offers of those free seeds which Hugh Low and Henry Ridley tried to press upon them, had gone to seek their fortunes elsewhere, without foreseeing the advent of that "devil carriage" motor-car. The Federated Malay States Handbook says that, by the end of 1905, the Peninsula could boast 1,480 miles of "metalled cart road", well bridged and suitable for any description of wheeled traffic – bullock-carts, gharries (though, "A journey in one of these vehicles not infrequently partakes of the nature of violent exercise," the writer warns), rickshaws, bicycles and, of course, cars.

The first automobile imported into the Malay States was a De Dion Motor Quadricycle and within six years, "Roots, Venables, Albions, Locomobile Steam Cars, Rambler petrol cars, Oldsmobiles, Serpollets, Darracqs, Siddeleys, Stars, Duryeas, Argylls", among others, raised a dust between the dark jungle trees, though with sufficient infrequency for the villagers to run from their *kampongs* to watch them bowl by. Few of the cars were more than eight horse-power, though the petrol-driven omnibuses that carried the mails to Pahang were equipped with sixteen horse-power engines. Conway Belfield, Resident of Selangor and author of the Handbook, suggests that Albions or De Dions were the best for Malayan driving, and that, due to the climate, all cars should be fitted with some form of cape, hood or canopy with a glass weather screen. The canopy, though it could be buttoned down all round the car, thus converting it into a perfectly weatherproof closed carriage, then "presents the disadvantage that the occupants of the car feel comparatively shut in when driving after sunset – just the time when the car is requisitioned as a means of obtaining fresh air". Belfield also discusses the question of solid versus pneumatic tyres and suggests a nice British compromise – pneumatic on the front and solid on the rear, as the "front tyres are seldom punctured, while pneumatics are easier to steer by".

The demand for rubber tyres, more than any other single item, triggered off the first Malayan rubber boom. Or, as Richard Winstedt expresses it in his original fashion, "It was in 1905 while I was in charge of the Land Office, Tapah, that the words Para Rubber were whispered in Wall Street and Mincing Lane and immediately evicted more tree spirits from Malayan forests than had ever been evicted during the previous two thousand years by Om, the Hindu word of power. Implacable as an army going into battle, Malays and Chinese started to fell the jungle, at first for the white man and then for themselves, hacking the way as surely as an invading conqueror for an industrial civilization such as Malaya had never known."

Henry Ridley at last came into his own. It was he who perfected an improved method of tapping which extracted the maximum of latex with the minimum of damage to the trees, and conducted other painstaking experiments, in conjunction with the new Department of Agriculture in Kuala Lumpur, on the advantages of morning rather than afternoon tapping, the best type of knife to use, the distances at which trees should be planted, the pros and cons of "clean-weeding" the ground beneath them. By 1908 rubber was being planted in every State of the Peninsula and there was a rush to buy up new land; the location of most big estates depended mainly on ease of access to main roads and railways– which meant that four-fifths of the total planted was in the more developed west, while Pahang and the other east coast states, lacking good communication routes and a willing labour force, again lost out.

In addition to the geographical imbalance, two other trends emerged at this time which were to cause trouble later: the rubber industry was gaining a dangerous economic dominance which made the country too dependent on fluctuations in world prices, and it was falling increasingly under European control. Resident Belfield, for example, in the same year that he wrote the States Handbook, issued a directive to the effect that no land abutting a government road should be "alienated to a native" without his sanction. "I am attempting," he added, "to concentrate native gardeners in specific areas and to discourage the occupation by them of land which may be usefully reserved for scientific planting" – which was usually the most profitable land.

Naturally, foreign planters and speculators, thus blessed with a little capital and much government encouragement, were quick to take advantage of the position and, as Winstedt wrote about his own Tapah district, the opening of so many large and new rubber estates, "destroyed the cobwebs in the local Land Office as it did in the great forest. Gone for ever, though we did not know it then, were the placid days when a Land Officer had done his duty if he took a gun and strolled through the fields looking for snipe to shoot and tardy rice-planters to cajole and threaten. Many of the snipe grounds were soon to be drained and even in rice-swamps Para rubber stumps were to be planted."

They grew, flourished, proliferated over the west coast landscapes – "A heavy bilious shade of green is this 'Amazonian weed' though its foliage as seen against the sky forms a comely outline," wrote another able M.C.S. cadet, Victor Purcell. "But when regimented in rows, geometrically straight and separated from one another by equal distances creating dark, prison-like galleries, it can be an eye-sore – even a threat"; also a promise of prosperity for some as, for the first time, British capital investment was attracted to the Peninsula on a really large scale. But those who made the money were the big companies that could afford to span the seven years between the first planting and the first tapping – such as the Petaling Rubber Estates Syndicate which paid a dividend to its shareholders of 45 per cent in 1908 and 325 per cent in 1910. For the small-holding Malay farmers feats like these were impossible; they remained in the *kampongs*, implacably resistant to the claims of modern capitalism, growing their cheap cash crops on the ground left to them after the rubber barons had marched their ranks of Amazonian weed across the landscapes.

The ranked trees still line the roads along which I drove in my hired white Vauxhall north to Taiping – "'The Town of Everlasting Peace', the name it was given at the end of the Chinese Clan Wars in 1874," notes a current guidebook. From the town's outskirts a narrow road leads 4,000 feet up to the summit of Maxwell Hill where cooling breezes stir the heads of familiar flowers – petunias, marigolds, begonias, lupins – that bloom in the gardens of the various bungalows. The dwellings look rather dilapidated with torn net curtains, peeling paint, a few rickety bamboo chairs on the verandahs, but each one still has its evocative name: "Hugh Low's Nest", "Treacher's Box" and "Speedy's Cottage".

The Indian Superintendent, who has lived there about forty years, told me that, in the good old days, there was a dairy on the Hill with Friesians and Jerseys and, at five o'clock every morning, a chap had to run down carrying bottles of fresh cream for the breakfast porridge of the officers stationed in the town below. There used to be a croquet lawn, tennis courts and a small market-garden too; but these are now overgrown. There's still a little wooden "belvedere" perched on a solitary peak and from it the view: straight rail-lines and the pools round the old tin workings shining in the sun; beyond, the Straits of Malacca, also shining, and cargo boats plying north towards Penang. William Edward Maxwell, whose Hill it is, would have enjoyed that view, with its evidence of so much directed and purposeful activity.

Down the Hill, merged into the view, I visited the Perak Museum Library and discovered that, in 1888, the omnibus left Taiping at seven a.m. for the base of the Hill and tickets could be purchased from Messrs Hong Bee & Co in the main square. That same year Resident Low ordered that all the brothels in Taiping should be confined to Market Street and Kota Road, that the coconut trees near the river should be burned to contain a plague of beetles, that "any officer employed under the Government of the State who becomes pecuniarily embarrassed from imprudence or other reprehensible cause will be removed from the Service". There is not much to tempt one into pecuniary embarrassment in

Taiping these days, I reflected as I drove off to Port Weld – named, of course, after the late Sir Frederick.

Weld was a fairly elderly man when he became Governor of the Straits Settlements in 1880. Though he suffered from gout and found the climate trying, he did not allow this to curtail his enthusiastic exploration of the Native States, but he sometimes flagged a little over his social duties in Singapore. At the Queen's Birthday Ball that first summer, for instance, he found that pain "mingled largely" with his pleasure in the proceedings. "I was in Court Dress," he explained to his friend, Lieutenant-Governor Anson, "and consequently obliged to wear pumps. Now the only pair I had came lately from England and what with the heat of the patent leather, they hurt my feet to such a degree that I had to go and sit by the billiard table behind a screen with the Maharaja and take them off." However it was all worth it. "My girls danced all night and were very happy indeed."

Weld would have taken little pleasure in his namesake port today. The railway runs through its centre and the houses on both sides look as if they are on the wrong side of the tracks. There is a stink of old rubber, dried fish and decaying fruit; scrawny dogs and hens scavenge among the refuse thrown along the drains. An elderly, dirty woman was bent over a sewing machine in the open door of "Sun Tit, Tailors" and another nearby was sweeping sawdust into piles – hopelessly, for the children following me scattered them as they passed. Some of the kids seemed unfriendly and called "Hello white woman" after me, which is very unusual for the country. I looked for the past: a railway sign for Port Weld in florid script like that of some English country station-halt where hollyhocks are grown by the station-master; a shack with Billiard Room over the door and a few men clicking balls about inside; a concrete hut for Port Weld Local Council. The place looks like an administrative mistake which peters out towards the steamy mangrove swamps and the flat sea beyond – a dull, tinny glare of water and old corrugated roofs. I was glad to drive away, the children stared at the car and shouted after me something which they obviously considered both funny and rude.

143

That was my furthest point north. I drove back through Taiping and so to Kuala Kangsa, a sleepy, attractive town with the brightly gilded onion-domed Ubudiah Mosque overlooking the Perak River. The town also contains the "oldest rubber tree in West Malaysia" according to a notice board placed in front of a gnarled and bushy tree on the hill – the sole survivor of the original dozen planted by Hugh Low in the Residency grounds. Long before the momentous advent of rubber, young Frank Swettenham spent the night of 1st November 1875 in Kuala Kangsa, he recorded in the journal that he kept during his trip. He left the village, as it then was, very early the next morning, stopped for breakfast at a small settlement where he asked the headman the usual details about local affairs and then carried on down-river to a place called Blanja.

Here the leisurely and detached tone of the journal changes abruptly. Swettenham picked up a pencil and wrote firmly and quickly in larger handwriting: "Four p.m. We have just reached Blanja and Jaji Ali has come to say Mr Birch and sixteen others were killed at Pasir Salak ... They are waiting now at Pasir Salak for me. They say I am ten times worse than Mr Birch." Tactics were discussed and the journal ends: "I will leave this book with the man of the boat who would rather not go in case I should not get through to Singapore ... but D.V. we will go for them yet, anyhow, I can't turn back." Well, he got through of course and the boatman took good care of the journal, which is now in the National Archives where I was able to hold it in my hands.

I discovered that a girls' school now stands on the small hill where Hugh Low's first Residency was sited and from it one can look along the wide sweep of the Perak River, which is satisfyingly the same. A thin wooden boat creeps hesitantly out on to the pale gold of the late afternoon waters and I hear distantly that old rhythmic splash of a paddle. I open one of my very favourite books, Isabella Bird's *The Golden Chersonese*, and read how, at the end of a long day's excursion into the jungle on the back of Low's Royal Elephant, she "came down upon the lovely Perak, which we crossed in a dug-out so nearly level with the water that at every

144

stroke of the paddle of the native who crouched in the bow, the water ran in over the edge. We landed at the village of Kuala Kangsa,

'In the glory of the sunset,
In the purple mists of evening'

in which the magnified purple mountains were piled like Alps against the flaming clouds. By the river-bank lay the Dragon boat and the square bamboo floating bath through the side of which Mr Birch was mortally wounded."

That was four years after Birch's assassination; presumably the bath was preserved as a memorial – and a reminder to the people of their misdeeds and the retribution that followed. The Dragon boat was still river-worthy because Low apparently offered Isabella Bird the use of it. On landing that evening, she continues, "We met a very bright intelligent-looking young Malay with a train of followers, a dandy almost in white trousers, short red sarong, black *baju* with gold buttons, gold watchguard and red head-dress. The expression on his face keen and slightly scornful. This is Raja Idris, a judge, and probable successor to the Perak throne."

Idris always like to cut a dash obviously – splendid in violet satin for the meeting of the State Council that M. de Saint-Pol Lias witnessed, and splendid again in 1903 when he arrived for luncheon in his motor-car, wearing, says Winstedt, "A dark blue European uniform, a sash of sacred yellow from waist to knee as became a good Muslim and a purple forage cap with the white feathers of a Civil Servant's cocked hat, a costume that made the best of all the worlds in which he and his forebears had lived, Hindu, Islamic, British".

The light was purpling towards evening as I went down the hill to the car. There's still a sweet sense of charm and peace about Kuala Kangsa which makes one reluctant to go. Isabella Bird, too, hated to leave; sitting on the comfortable verandah of the Residency she wrote, "This is my last evening here and I am so sorry. It is truly 'the wilds'. There is rest. Then the apes are delightful companions, and there are all sorts of beasts and birds and creeping things from elephants downwards . . . I like Kuala Kangsa better

145

than any place that I have been in Asia and am proportionately sorry to leave it." But she had to.

The next morning she was up early, ready to take off on Hugh Low's pony with its English saddle and the Royal Elephant to carry her luggage. "It was absurd," she wrote, "to see the huge beast lie down merely to receive my little valise and canvas roll, with a small accumulation of Malacca canes, mats, krisses, tigers' teeth and claws and an elephant's tusk, the whole not weighing a hundred pounds." Low was already working at his desk when she left, with Eblis, who was ailing, on his lap and the bully Mahmoud on a roof-beam glaring down. She had wanted to leave at four o'clock, before even Low had begun work, but, she noted, "There are so many tigers about just now in the jungle through which the road passes that it is not considered prudent for me to leave before six, when they will have retired to their lairs." I drove to the out-skirts of the town looking for a petrol station. There's one: "Put a Tiger in your Tank", reads the Esso sign. I took off, re-charged, in the direction of Kuala Lumpur.

Isabella Bird did not visit Yap Ah Loy's tin-mining settlement, which was a pity because she would have had some colourful comments to make about him, and he would probably have given her a grand welcome. His portrait, looking appropriately saintly, now graces the main altar in one of the city's largest Buddhist temples, and, in the National Museum, a number of faded-sepia photographs show the steamy, tatty, rickety, smelly little place as it was in his day. On the whole, the present inhabitants of Kuala Lumpur do not seem very interested in that, or in other details of their "colonial past", and the old street names which are vibrant with meaning for the historically-minded have been carefully expunged. Swettenham, Maxwell and Clifford all had stately roads around the pleasant Lake Gardens named after them; there was also a Treacher Road, a Weld Supermarket, Birch Road (in memoriam) and Syers Road – after the noble Commissioner of Police who was gored to death in 1897 when hunting a particu-larly vicious seladang. Along the roads, the stately Siddeleys, Hum-bers and Venables rolled, carrying the senior administrators to their desks in the Secretariat, their wives to bridge parties and charity fairs – for, by the 1920s, Kuala Lumpur was a comfortable, sociable place to live, for those with a good salary and a white skin.

To obtain a post in the Federal capital was usually a plum reserved for men with several years of service behind them; new recruits to the M.C.S. usually started in the hinterlands. I met one of them, Mervyn Sheppard, in the bar of Kuala Lumpur's Majestic Hotel – its high ceilings and fans, low leather chairs redolent of the Between-the-Wars period when it was built. Mr Sheppard told me that when he arrived in the country he was issued with a white drill coat and the regulation Perak Buttons and sent to an outpost in the interior where he worked for three months under a dour Scot who had been shell-shocked in the First World War and scarcely spoke to anyone. "One day," he continued, "I was sent out to collect rents on my bicycle in the old-fashioned way and I was in a little village school surrounded by people telling me about this and that, when there was a screech of brakes and a big black limousine with a British flag on the front drew up. A tall, bent Englishman, dressed in the usual regulation white duck, got out and started talking to the people in fluent Malay with a strong Pahang accent. They all listened and seemed to welcome what he said; then he got back in the car and drove himself away, without as much as acknowledging the existence of the callow young recruit – me – who stood staring at him . . ." Sheppard laughed. "That was just like Hugh Clifford," he concluded without malice. "It was always the ordinary natives first with him."

Clifford, whose interest in and affection for the Malays and their country remained deep and genuine, had been posted off to Trinidad and Tobago, nevertheless, when Swettenham retired in 1903. He had been bitter and grieved at the move, but Colonial Office logic was inscrutable and irrefutable and for the next twenty-four years he was given a variety of far-flung assignments – as Governor of the Gold Coast, of Nigeria and, later, of Ceylon. In 1927, when Mervyn Sheppard first saw him from a respectful distance, Sir Hugh Clifford, G.C.M.G., had at last been appointed Governor of the Straits Settlements and High Commissioner for the Malay States – the appointment which fulfilled his highest hopes, he said, and gave him more pleasure than any other, save for that first assignment as Sir Frederick Weld's trouble-shooter in Pahang in 1887.

And this was undoubtedly true, for, during his long years of exile from the Malayan scene, he continued to write obsessively about the country where he had spent his toughest, loneliest, happiest years – as his published works bear witness. *East Coast Etchings, The Further Side of Silence, Malayan Monochromes, In Court and Kampong* are unread, almost unreadable now, except for one as devoted to late nineteenth-century Malaya as Clifford was. Joseph Conrad, who became friendly with Clifford after he had left Malaya, praised the books for their detailed and loving observation of a little-known terrain, but was realistically non-committal about their lasting literary merit. Unfortunately, Conrad wrote, the author's own personality which was "of the greatest interest" is only "seen between the lines – like the progress of a traveller in the jungle that may be traced by the sound of the *parang* chopping the swaying creepers, while the man himself is glimpsed now and then, indistinct and passing between the trees".

I sought more first-hand memories of that elusive, ambivalent personality in a private room of the Majestic Hotel where his works are ranged along a shelf in faded yellow-ochre, washed-out beiges and blues with florid gold lettering – typical of the popular travel-books of the period produced to satisfy the globe-trotting dreams of the stay-at-home circulating-library reader. The room was occupied by Mrs Dorothy Nixon, the elderly widow of a rubber planter, who once ran the circulating library which was housed next to the Selangor Club on the green *padang* in Kuala Lumpur's centre, from which she used to dispatch boxes of thrillers and romances up-country to the excitement-starved planters' families.

Gentle, frail and rather vague, she sat in her comfortable chintz armchair and remembered, "Oh, the twenties ... when Clifford came back. We had a lot of fun in those days. There was 'Bu', the Sultan of Johore's son, we all called him 'Bu'. He was quite a character and very good at polo, but one had to keep him on the water-wagon before a match. He gave me his favourite polo pony once – after a match that he'd won because I made a pact with the barman to prevent him drinking any champagne beforehand, so it was really my victory, he said . . . But you asked about Hugh Clifford, such a nice kind man, very tall, but bent, he looked much older than he actually was, I believe. Mind you, he always had an eye for the ladies. I remember once, he'd been visiting the Sultan up-river, and he came down to our Estate for tea. And I'd rung up the other wives beforehand and said, 'Now, who is the prettiest new wife we have, because she must sit next to him?' So I left the seat next to her empty and, when Clifford arrived in his boat, all the ladies stood up to greet him, because he was the High Commissioner then, you know. And as he walked to the seat I'd reserved for him, he squeezed my arm and said, 'You are kind to me.' I'll never forget it, he was very gentlemanly and harmless, you realize, and I don't think his wife minded – she may have smacked his bottom occasionally!"

I left Mrs Nixon to her memories and returned to my own room in the Majestic Hotel, with its high ceiling, fan, cool red-tile floor, green shutters and cavernous bath with big brass taps. I ordered a gin and tonic on the 1930s-vintage house-phone and stood at the window looking out while I awaited its always tardy arrival. Two days previously I had met another of Malaya's long-resident ex-colonials, who could also remember Hugh Clifford. "I was only a nipper at the time, mind," he began hastily. "Clifford was a devout Catholic you know – came to our church every Sunday. He used to shuffle up to the front row, very slowly, all by himself. He always looked rather lonely and faraway, I thought, and he was strange somehow. There were stories that he used to go out late at night, all by himself, wearing an ordinary open shirt and flannels – no kind of uniform so that he wouldn't be recognized. And he'd sit at the open-air stalls and eat Malay *satay* and rice, which he said he liked better than all the official banquets. . . . Poor chap, he had to retire after only two years as High Commissioner, you know. 'Mad Clifford' they called him, at the end." That return as Commissioner had shattered his golden dream of the old rural Malaya which he had so lovingly cherished and described during his years of exile. As a modern historian has noted, "It was Swettenham who continued to fill the correspondence columns of *The Times* with letters about Malaya during the 1930s. Clifford had no more to say."

My gin and tonic arrived, brought by one of the Hotel's very elderly Chinese "boys", wearing wide black trousers and slapping across the tiles in his open-back slippers. I raised my glass to "mad Clifford", whose hopes were realized too late and whose uncertainties were never resolved; and to that young Hugh who took his daily constitutional around and around the only square in Pekan where he lived so self-consciously, uneasily, joyously. And I remembered, in my salutation, other monotonous and lonely constitutionals I had read about in the course of my excursion into the past: Emily Innes, treading Langat's mud path day after day, carrying her parasol high and counting the number of blue crabs in the slime below, because there was nothing else to do; an anonymous District Officer who, stuck in a Selangor village of the 1890s, "perambulated and re-perambulated" its main street, until he was "on intimate terms with the very dried fish in the shop-fronts, and at no loss to recognize, each in its accustomed place, the strange and varied effluvia which the languid breezes carry into the middle of the road – the fish, drains, decaying mangoes and, near the cemetery, the sickly-sweet perfume of frangipani ..."; and Hugh Low, with an ape on his shoulder, his retriever behind him, taking his habitual evening stroll through the gardens of the Kuala Kangsa Residency to look at the young coffee bushes and the rubber seedlings.

I raised my glass to him also, and to the eagle-eyed William Edward Maxwell whom few loved and most respected, and who perhaps knew a bit too much for his own good. And, with reservations, I saluted last the ambitious, ebullient Frank Athelstane Swettenham, who was always rather too big for his boots, and something of a wily bird, I've always thought. In the quick tropical sunset the swallows are skimming and screaming around the minarets of the "Arabesque Renaissance" folly that is Kuala Lumpur's railway-station. The homegoing commuter traffic thunders past it, and past the doors of the nearby National Museum wherein stands an impressively large bronze statue of

Swettenham, wearing his High Commissioner's uniform and his imperially cocked hat. He looks as stern and firm as ever; the "unrepentant imperialist" to the last, as one historian dubs him. Every day, groups of neatly-dressed school-children tour the museum and glance fleetingly up at him with their dark and lively eyes before passing on to more interesting native-cultural exhibits.

12

The colonial legacy

Malaysia is a country I find difficult to leave alone, and I have always intuitively understood why so many of my compatriots loved and love it. It is culturally complex, politically fairly tense, economically rather uncertain, but there is an easy and unaggressive sense of acceptance about its people – born to enforced tolerance, they have developed a wry awareness of human limitations that many bigger and bolder nations have unfortunately lost. And the land is so very beautiful: the manageable, tamed beauty of its colonial fringes – coasts, hill-stations, small towns; the exuberant wildernesses of its interiors where almost totally unexplored areas of rainforest have existed in their primary, undisturbed state for about a hundred million years.

Here, ragged canopies of trees, some over two hundred feet high, range in uneven ridges over the highlands, sprawl and intertwine over the lowlands and marshy swamps, the dense masses of vegetation checked only by the passage of the wide rivers – except in one or two areas where the taming of the jungle is still going forward. In the summer of 1975 I stood on one such spot – a small hill in south-east Pahang, surrounded by thousands of acres of tropical rainforest. This particular hill was remarkable because it had a name – Bukit Ridan – and was one of several in the vicinity that had recently been cleared of its dense vegetation so that its pitted, pinkish soil was exposed like raw flesh to the rays of the hot sun, the slashes of the torrential afternoon rains. Three bulldozers, ineffectual yellow ants, were industriously trying to push further away the thick jungle tangles, which, in all the near distances, were already threatening to claw back over the bared soil.

By my side, the Chinese contractor employed to clear the site described the future to me with airy waves of his arm: "Golf course there one day and park for people. Big offices over there, on made-up hill, lots of men at the desks." He grinned. "Airport further out, see – over there – and big highway coming in near. Houses up hill, all separate, very fine, brick maybe. Low ones, bungalows, near swamp down there. Very bad ground . . ." He grinned again. "Don't buy one!" Considering the difficulties of construction and transport, I wondered whether it was necessary to build on several levels in this way. "Stupid," he said, shrugging. "Planners' idea. Why not all on one flat place? Straight streets, houses all-alike, little offices. Make it all easy, quick and cheap. This only a jungle town."

But Bukit Ridan is not in the least intended to be one of those easy-come-easy-go shanty towns propped up with jungle-rollers and woven with thatch, its drains stinking and its tracks sloshy, in the manner of old Kuala Lumpur. On the contrary, the Development Scheme for Pahang Tenggara, part of what the planners call Malaysia's "region of opportunity" and of which Bukit Ridan will form the prestigious centre, is intended to extend over some two and a half million acres within the next twenty years. About half a million people are expected to go and settle there, living, say the planners, in "processing and basic service communities" of about ten thousand population, and "service and supply towns" of twice that size, and the "regional centre" of Bukit Ridan, with a projected population of seventy thousand by 1990.

The settlers will cultivate the land and fell the valuable timber, staff the schools and hospitals, sit in their air-conditioned offices and watch with pleasure as the planes come hurtling along the new runways, the cars along the new highways. And, after work, the high wage-earners among them will return to their brick-and-concrete houses on the hills, for, in the Malay mind, the traditional wood-and-thatch bungalow is but a *kampong*-house, fit only for the peasantry. All in all, an enthusiastic Malay academic told me, the Pahang Tenggara Development is going to be "one of the

153

most ambitious large-scale exercises in social engineering any-where in South-East Asia." Certainly it is the sort of clean sheet that delighted British colonialists and entrepreneurs a hundred years ago. "If it doesn't work," a planning official told me, "we can't blame it all on the past any more. We've told the officers responsible, 'At the end of the time, we'll either decorate you or line you up against the wall and shoot the lot of you!'"

He was joking, but there is a lot of national pride as well as money invested in the Scheme – as I saw when I visited other development sites where the future has taken a slightly firmer hold. First to MARDI (the Malaysian Research and Development Institute) housed in a low white building amid cultivated fields where a number of enthusiastic young agriculturists are experimenting with the growing of sago in swamp conditions, and of tropical fruits and tea, the latter, at present in its nursery stages, under the customary tender care of Indian workers. Till recently, the large-scale government-financed agricultural developments have depended on rubber and oil-palm as the major resource crops. But world prices of the former are still extremely unreliable and the latter has the nasty habit of keeping one labourer busy on every ten acres for the first four years of its life, after which fifteen acres can be managed easily by one man – and that leaves half a man jobless, as it were. So more crop diversification in order to create a greater variety of jobs is a key factor, which is why MARDI workers are experimenting with new ways of canning and pickling papaya, guava, jack-fruit and soursop, of growing more guinea-grass for the buffalo (whose mortality from malnutrition is at present high), of breeding commercial quantities of trout and prawn in their artificial ponds.

I was then driven by Land-Rover to DARABIF (DARA is the name of the catalysing government agency, "bif" is Malay for beef) where experiments are going forward to improve local cattle stocks by inter-breeding them with Australian animals. The idea of producing top quality beef for the table is fairly new to the Malays, who customarily make very good curries from very elderly cows. So there's a lot to be done in the way of finding out exactly how many acres of lush, damp, seven-foot-high grass will support each animal, and how vulnerable the new breeds will be to the local varieties of cattle parasite and other tropical infections.

DARABIF headquarters is an equatorial version of a Texan ranch. Malay farmhands move slowly and quietly about sheds filled with sacks of fertilizers, skeins of rope and cotton waste, machine parts, fencing posts and rolls of barbed wire; they sport jungle-boots, jeans and wide-awake straw hats, but they ride on motor-bikes, not horses, to feed the cattle, for tyres are less prone to foot-rot than hooves in this damp warm grass. I am told of the occasional marauding raid on the cattle by tiger and wild boar, but there is no serious threat from the remaining wild life. The few people living in the region already subsist on a low-protein diet and, when their numbers increase as the Development progresses, it seems they can be relied upon to kill off any remaining protein-rich wild animals, in spite of conservationists' efforts. In this and other ways the teeming-alive forests that so enchanted Hugh Clifford a hundred years ago are being tamed, as the tin and rubber barons once clipped and regimented the jungles of the Peninsula's west coast.

Back in Bukit Ibam, the Development's largest town to date, there is a strong sense of the pioneering frontier, a certain piquant insecurity of human tenure that has not been quite banished yet – as it has so thoroughly from even the remotest English village. The settlement comprises rows of shabby, "railway-style" shacks for the labourers, newly-built hostels for the young single workers, bungalows, with verandahs and bougainvillaea bushes on tough-grass little lawns, for the managers, and one of each of most of the essentials – a school, a hospital, a public works department, a large store, and a rest-house with mosquito nets shrouding spartan bedsteads. There is also one television set in its common-room round which the locals gather in the evenings to drink tea and Coca-Cola and glean the latest flickerings from the outer world.

Even the affairs of Kuala Lumpur seem pretty remote from this vantage point – sixty miles to the nearest surfaced road and no way to it except over rutted and rain-sodden lumber tracks. So most of the workers are more or less marooned for the term of their short contracts. Many of the young women are engaged in the first light industry – a "jade factory" where they polish the second-quality green stones mined in the area to a lustre sufficiently jade-ish for the adornment of made-in-Japan table-lighters. The men supervise the planting of crops, felling of timber, constructing of roads and drains.

Many of them show a sense of adventure and commitment, especially the young technicians who are trying to put in workable practice the numerous and sometimes contradictory estimates, diagrams, instructions and analyses made by the faraway consultants, scientists, engineers, sociologists. For the whole project, I was told, has always suffered a glut of remote expertise and planning, a dearth of practical on-the-spot talent and drive. The trained few working in Bukit Ibam are the privileged, recently home-grown equivalents of the self-confident British cadets of the Malayan Civil Service who used suddenly to arrive on some patch of raw terrain with their plans and survey instruments and dreams for a more prosperous future. And they too are content to live in frugal dedication for a while, watching the land accept the people. And in due course, I suppose, most of those young technicians will grow plumper and more luxury-loving and seek postings in the offices of the urban Public Works Departments where all the maps and diagrams on the walls reduce everything to apparent and immediate manageability.

The next day I was driven the sixty miles out by Land-Rover through the pinky sludge, past the neat rows of nursery tea-bushes, small fields of bananas and sugarcane islanded between swamps of sword-sharp lelang grass and jungle-deep hills. Occasionally we passed a lay-by with a thatched stall selling jungle fruits to the lumber truckers, and tracts of recently-cleared land, the trees hacked out and mostly burned, but for a few lop-sided ashy stumps stuck in pools of mud – the whole looking as decimated and melancholy, even under the clear blue sky, as a World War I scarred battlefield. Once our vehicle reached the tarmac road lined with villages, each with its police-box and bus-stop, it seemed barely credible that the Pahang Tenggara Development actually existed – locked away inside that hot, damp, empty interior.

At Pekan, where Hugh Clifford once played billiards with the sprigs of the Pahang nobility and where, reputedly, the "wickedest man in Asia" once kept Sir Frederick Weld and his entourage waiting while he finished a game of dice, I boarded a local bus and headed northwards up the coast for a way. In the manner of most countries that we of the West are pleased to call "underdeveloped", there was a constant and mysterious interchange of people from one village to another. They carried cloth bundles, battered suitcases tied with string, plastic bags stuffed with pineapples, eggs, dried fish. They got off leisurely and strolled away into the seeming middle of nowhere along dusty paths among the mangrove or sugarcane. Everyone seemed to know what they would be doing for the rest of that day, that it would not be too burdensome or rushed, that tomorrow would be very similar.

To an extent, the cliché, much beloved by Clifford, that this slow-paced, small-scale rural scene is the "real Malaya" still holds good: even today about eighty per cent of the people live in settlements of less than five thousand. And, "To visit the soul of Malaysia one should visit the East Coast," say the travel brochures, where, according to outsiders anyway, the people are still proud and touchy, indolent and generous and many of the older generation think of themselves as Pahangese first, Malaysian second. They fish, grow paddy, sell their coconuts, yams, bamboo shoots in the local markets, cut wood from the mangrove swamps to burn in large kilns for charcoal. Their setting is idyllic: hot white-sand beaches glinting in the sun, fringed with golden-green palms and dotted with bleached-wood fishing boats; between sea and road, clumps of their tattily thatched houses-on-stilts.

I spent a night in one. At sunset, the family sprawl on soft straw mats on the deep verandah while the evening meal is cooked at the "kitchen end" over a charcoal fire. I was offered boiled crabs, stringy chicken in a thin yellow curry sauce, glutinous rice-balls wrapped in banana leaves, cooked cucumbers and sugary cakes of dyed pink coconut and fermented peanuts. My bed was a red silk quilt behind a lattice screen off the main room; next door lay the family's blind "granny", her wizened frame wrapped in a sun-faded sarong. I was told that she could well remember being carried over unbridged rivers on a hired man's back when she once made the journey to distant Kuala Lumpur, and the great local excitement when the first aeroplane winged in from the South China Sea and nobody knew what it was. Naturally it was taken as an evil omen, and women of such advanced years are still apt to work up a state of alarm if they see a flight of birds flying over the roof in the wrong direction at the wrong season. "Granny's" niece, whose guest I was, could remember the next sequence of events impinging from the outside world: the Japanese occupation, when there were Indian children starving in the market place and one was never allowed out alone for fear of being raped by Japanese soldiers; later British jeeps thundered along the road past the village, full of soldiers with guns at the ready.

Before I went to sleep that night I listened to the sounds of chickens, goats and dogs rattling in the refuse under the house, of frogs in the ditches, of owls in the mangroves, of bats (or rats) rustling in the thatch above, and I thought about other people's memories. In the morning, the first sounds were of a cock crowing directly beneath my bed, or so it seemed, and someone shredding coconut on the kitchen-verandah by drawing the shell across a large iron grater with crocodile-sharp teeth. And I thought how Emily Innes' every boring dawn would have begun with such sounds, and how she must have yearned for some hint of Western-style bustle, some unexpected reverberations as proof of a world beyond the mud flats.

For my part, having the luxury of mobility, I was reluctant to leave, especially as I had been told that the beautiful beach nearby was destined to become the site of a splendid new multi-million dollar, multi-storey tourist "complex" that would attract thousands of visitors from Australia, America and Japan. They will arrange their long slim bodies on the hot white sands (yes, even the affluent young Japanese are usually long-limbed now), they will buy woven mats and shell necklaces from the quaint natives in the nearby village and, each evening, they will sink their strong well-cared-for teeth into the succulent steaks that will be sent to their tables from the flourishing ranches of the Pahang hinterlands. It is all doomed to work successfully I thought, assailed by a

Cliffordian-type romanticism for the changeless native pastoral, as I boarded an express bus for Kuala Lumpur.

In Kuala Lumpur itself the vestiges of jungle-green are being carefully expunged and many of the classic Western planners' mistakes have already been expensively made. There are too many concrete-and-glass hotels belonging to those chains that link the cities of the world in their brand of plush and banal "internationalism". So many are there, the joke goes, that the next one will have to be built on one of the city's remaining roundabouts and will be reached by walking across the roofs of the choked mass of vehicles that always ring its perimeter. Though congestion is endemic, the claims of the traffic are paramount and, along the main roads, pedestrians perch precariously on narrow raised ridges down the centres, waiting to dodge across between the streams of ever-oncoming cars. In the suburbs, blocks of low-cost housing and crass concrete shopping complexes have been plonked, as hard-edged and charmless as those on the fringes of our own Midland cities.

But, naturally enough, most young Malaysians do not see it like that. For them, the Kuala Lumpur of today is as glamorous and promise-packed as New York was in the 1920s to the hick from the mid-West. It is a vigorous city therefore, the thousands of passing-by lithe young bodies and unlined optimistic faces a queasy reminder to the approaching-middle-aged Westerner that, in South-East Asia, more than two-thirds of the population is under thirty. But it will be difficult, as the planners admit, to tempt enough of these young back to such jungle hinterlands as Pahang now they have seen the flashy lights of the capital and nurtured sky-high and often unrealistic expectations of their glittering futures.

For the pattern of the past has been that the brightest village children, who managed to secure an education beyond the basic secondary level, made for the towns and seldom returned. As a senior Ministry official remarked when I was asking him about the Pahang Tenggara Scheme, "Look what happened to me – I left my *kampong* when I was was fourteen . . . I go back occasionally and look at the tree I used to climb . . . But nostalgia like that is no good now for my generation, we have invested our brains and money elsewhere. That's what wrong with rural Malaysia." The hope is that, in the new, government-sponsored rural developments, a more adventurous pioneering spirit linked to a greater feeling of inter-community participation will develop and will cut through the present tight kinship loyalties that are based on race, culture and language. "We can only try this in places like the Pahang Tenggara," the man from the Ministry said, "where all the settlers will be strangers to each other and they'll be more adaptable because they've actually made the move to go and live there."

This situation is, of course, part of the country's "colonial legacy", for the British, throughout most of their rule, did not do enough to improve the educational standards of the ordinary stay-at-home people, nor did they seek to instil any sense of national unity among the various racial groups. Indeed their influence was often divisive (most of the administrators remained either "pro-Malay" or "pro-Chinese") and, even after Federation, they did not take the political and economic initiatives required to give the whole Peninsula one national identity.

During the Colony's golden pre-World War II days, upper-class Malays, Chinese and Indians, who had mostly been sent abroad for an English public-school education, mixed socially with the ruling British, learned to play all the English games, on the sports field and in the drawing-room, and spoke fluent English. It is still the case today therefore that when a Malay, a Chinese and an Indian meet in a restaurant they talk together in English because it is their only common tongue. This is a situation which the Government is determined to change, and the strains and confusions over its implementation of Bahasa Malaysia as the nation's official language clearly illustrate the tensions that exist beneath the surface.

It is intended that, by 1985, Bahasa Malaysia will be the official medium of instruction throughout the educational system, whereas, in the past, the principal teaching medium could be either Malay, Chinese, Tamil or English. However, many non-Malays – that is, Chinese, Indians and other indigenous races including those in

Sabah and Sarawak – greatly resent this measure. This is not only because their children will be educated in what is, to them, essentially a second language, but because, whatever its apologists say, Bahasa Malaysia is a culturally restricted and technically impoverished language compared to both English and Chinese. There is therefore the need to invent a large number of "modern" Bahasa words which, incidentally, have a cumulatively unsettling effect on the native English speaker so that, after a while, I began to wonder if I had taken leave of my spelling senses. *Sekola* for school, *teksi* for taxi, *talivisen* for television, *sikal* for cycle and *motokar* for car are some of the more decipherable examples; the recent introduction of *seksi* for section has caused some amusement in the various sections of the British High Commission.

The implementation of Bahasa Malaysia is fundamental to the government's determination to Malayanize Malaysia – culturally, economically, socially. It also means in practice that the Malays (the *bumiputras*, that is, "the sons of the soil") are given every possible educational and financial encouragement to get ahead in all the professional and commercial fields, even when they are not very competent, and often at the expense of the other races. However, this subject is so highly emotive that I was several times warned not to write about it at all. If I did, and said the wrong things, I was told that I might find myself on one of the Immigration Officers' long black lists if I ever wanted to return to the country.

That is one good reason for leaving the subject alone; another is that I was not in the country long enough to do more than gather up a few shreds – of fact, fantasy, fury – about it. However, that I was given such serious warnings points up one basic truth about Malaysian society today: it does not enjoy the same degree of freedom that still exists in most countries of Western Europe. And having said so much, I remember the conflict and upheaval that has been caused in the past by comparing and confusing Asian concepts of "freedom" and "justice" with Western ones.

The men who helped to create the Malaya of the past were seldom prey to such doubts and their certainties made them effective. They were not all, as fervent anti-colonists have since labelled them, "financial adventurers and well-connected freebooters whose machinations in the Sultans' courts sealed the fate of Malaya for eighty years"; nor, on the other hand, were they the spreaders of so much moral and social sweetness and light as they themselves supposed. They were, by any colonial standards, conscientious and responsible administrators and their concern for the Malay people was, for the most part, genuine and deep, even though many of them were guilty of that brand of paternalistic condescension which, today, has made writers like Richard Winstedt particularly unpopular.

But this is of merely academic concern. For, though colonialism is generally discredited, Malaysians as a whole seem to have emerged from the experience without harbouring much bitterness. Of course, their politicians worry a great deal about the country's political and economic relationship with the Western world, but Britain is not a special target for abuse. And the names of the men who started to tame the Malayan jungles in the cause of "civilization", "justice" and "progress" seem now but faintly chiselled on the national consciousness, as the first name among them is still indistinctly embedded in a certain granite memorial that stands on the river-bank in the village of Pasir Salak: "Here at the fort of Datok Maharaja Lela the Honourable J. W. Birch, First British Resident of Perak, was killed in the performance of his duty on 2nd November 1875."

Bibliography

I. *Official Records*

i. Parliamentary Papers:
C.1503, 1505, 1512 (1876)   Relating to the Malay States
C.2410 (1879)   Instructions to British Residents
C.3429 (1882)   Slavery in the Malay States
C.7227 (1893)   Reports on the Malay States
ii. State Secretariat Files for Selangor (1875–80)
State Secretariat Files for Perak (1876–82)
State Secretariat Files for Pahang (1888–95)
iii. Perak Circulars for 1888 and 1893
Selangor Government Gazette, 1890–92
Annual Reports, Perak, 1874–79

II. *Journals, Newspapers, Unpublished Sources*

(J.M.B.R.A.S. = *Journal of Malay Branch of Royal Asiatic Society*)
(J.S.B.R.A.S. = *Journal of Straits Branch of Royal Asiatic Society*)

Allen, J. deV., "Two Imperialists", J.M.B.R.A.S., 1964
Chew, E., "Sir Frank Swettenham and the Federation of the Malay States", *Modern Asian Studies*, 1968
Clifford, Hugh, Diary of, Pahang, 1888, 1893
Clifford, Hugh, "Life in the Malay Peninsula", *Proceedings of Royal Colonial Institute*, 1898
Gullick, J. M., "Captain Speedy of Larut", J.M.B.R.A.S., 1953
——"Kuala Lumpur 1880–95", J.M.B.R.A.S., 1955
——"A Careless Heathen Philosopher", J.M.B.R.A.S., 1953
Innes, James, Letter Book and Journal, 1882–85
Linehan, W., "A History of Pahang", J.M.B.R.AS., 1936

Mallal, M. A., "J. W. Birch, The Causes of his Assassination", Thesis, University of Malaysia, 1952

Maxwell, W. E., "Laws and Customs of the Malays", J.S.B.R.AS., 1884

—— "Malay Proverbs", J.S.B.R.AS., 1883

—— "Laws Relating to Slavery", J.S.B.R.A.S., 1890

Middlebrook, S. M., "Yap Ah Loy", J.M.B.R.A.S., 1951

Penang Gazette, Numbers for 1886, 1892

Sadka, Emily (ed.), "Journal of Sir Hugh Low 1877", J.M.B.R.A.S., 1954

Selangor Journal, Numbers for 1892–96

Straits Produce Magazine, Numbers for 1894, 1895

Straits Times, Numbers published in 1876, 1880, 1889, 1903

Stratton-Brown, Mrs W., "Long Ago in Selangor", MS., Rhodes Library, 1896

Swettenham, Frank, "Journal of Journey across the Malay Peninsula", J.S.B.R.A.S., 1885

—— Journal, 1874–75, National Archives, Malaysia

—— "The Independent States of the Malay Peninsula", J.S.B.R.AS., 1880

—— "Perak Journals", ed. C. Cowan, J.M.B.R.A.S., 1951

Sheppard, M. C., "Clifford of Pahang", *Straits Times Annual*, 1956

Winstedt, R. O., "History of Perak", J.M.B.R.A.S., 1934

—— "History of Selangor", J.M.B.R.AS., 1934

III. *Published Books*

Anson, A. E., *About Myself and Others*, London, 1920

Bastin, J. and Winks, R., *Malaysia, Selected Historical Readings*, London, 1966

Bastin, J. and Roolvink, R., *Malaysian and Indonesian Studies*, Oxford, 1964

Belfield, Conway, *Handbook of Federated Malay States*, 1906

Bird, Isabella, *The Golden Chersonese*, London, 1883

Chai, Hon-Chan, *The Development of British Malaya*, London, 1964

Clifford, Hugh, *East Coast Etchings,* Singapore, 1896

——*Studies in Brown Humanity*, London, 1898

—— *In Court and Kampong*, London, 1897

—— *Malayan Monochromes*, London, 1913

—— *The Further Side of Silence*, London, 1916

—— *In Days that are Dead*, London, 1926

—— *Bushwhacking*, London, 1929
Comber, L. F., *Chinese Secret Societies in Malaya*, New York, 1959
Conrad, Joseph, *Notes on Life and Letters*, London, 1921
Cowan, C. D., *Nineteenth-Century Malaya*, London, 1961
Doyle, P., *Tin Mining in Larut*, London, 1879
Gullick, J. M., *Indigenous Political Systems of W. Malaysia*, London, 1958
Hall, H. H., *The Colonial Office*, London, 1937
Hornaday, W. T., *Two Years in the Jungle*, New York, 1880
Innes, Emily, *The Chersonese with the Gilding Off*, London, 1885
Jackson, J., *Planters and Speculators*, Kuala Lumpur, 1966
Jackson, R. N., *Pickering*, Kuala Lumpur, 1965
Kennedy, J., *A History of Malaya*, London, 1962
Lias, Brau de Saint-Pol, *Perak et les Orang-Sakeys: Voyage dans l'interieur de la presqu'île Malaise*, Paris, 1883
Loh, Philip, *The Malay States, 1877–95*, Singapore, 1969
Lovat, Alice, *The Life of Sir Frederick Weld*, London, 1924
Low, Hugh, *Sarawak, Its Inhabitants and Productions*, London, 1848
McNair, J. F., *Perak and the Malays*, London, 1878
Makepeace, W., *One Hundred Years of Singapore*, London, 1921
Maxwell, P. B., *Our Malay Conquests*, London, 1878
Miller, H., *The Story of Malaysia*, London, 1965
Parkinson, Northcote, *British Intervention in Malaya*, Singapore, 1960
Pope-Hennessy, J., *Verandah*, London, 1964
Purcell, V., *Memoirs of a Malayan Official*, London, 1965
Rathborne, A., *Camping and Tramping in Malaya*, London, 1898
Roff, W. R., *The Origins of Malay Nationalism*, New Haven, 1967
Sadka, Emily, *The Protected Malay States*, Kuala Lumpur, 1968
Swettenham, F. A., *About Singapore*, 1893
—— *The Real Malay*, London, 1900
—— *Malay Sketches*, London, 1913
—— *British Malaya*, London, 1907
—— *Footprints in Malaya*, London, 1941
Thio, Eunice, *British Policy in the Malay Peninsula*, Kuala Lumpur, 1968
Thomson, J., *The Straits of Malacca, etc.*, 1875
Tregonning, K. G., *Papers on Malayan History*, Singapore, 1962
Winstedt, R. O., *A History of Malaya*, London, 1962
—— *Start from Alif: Count from One*, London, 1969

Index

Clifford *cont.*
   Malay States 147–9; memories
      of 148–50
coffee cultivation 92, 116, 130
Colborne, General Sir John 18, 19
Collectors and Magistrates (later
   District Officers) 27
Conrad, Joseph 148

Daly, Dominic 33, 63, 64
DARABIF 154–5
Davidson, James, Selangor Resident 23, 34
District Officers 105–6, 150
Douglas, Captain Bloomfield:
   Selangor Resident 23, 31–6,
   63–6; his Residency in Klang
   33; despotism and lack of
   judgment 33–6, 64–6; ceremony of reprimand 35; Residency in Kuala Lumpur 63;
   forced to resign 66–7
Dunlop, Captain 135
Durian Sabatang 88

East India Company 1–2
education 107–8, 160–1
Etam, Raja 35

Fairfield, Edward 119, 122
Federation 124–33; proposals for
   120–1; creation of 122–3; end of
   State Councils 125; specialist
   departments 125–6; Confer-
   ences (1897) 127–8, (1903) 131–2
Footprints in Malaya (Swettenham)
   114

Golden Chersonese, The (Bird)
   144–5

Gomback River 61

Hill, Heslop 92
hill stations 111–12, 142
Hornaday, William 33, 55
horticulture 88–9, 101

Idris, Raja 97; Sultan of Perak
   106, 127, 131–2, 136–7, 138–9,
   145
In Court and Kampong (Clifford)
   129, 148
industry 3, 40–3, 61, 63, 92, 100,
   156
Innes, Emily 27–9, 30–2, 88, 96,
   150, 158
Innes, James, Collector and Magistrate, Langat 27–8, 29–31, 34,
   65, 66, 96

Jervois, Sir William 11, 17, 18,
   19, 20, 21, 22, 24, 39

Klang 110; Residency 33, 35;
   rail link with Kuala Lumpur
   73
Klang River 61
Kuala Kangsa 14, 137–9; Residency 38, 47–9, 87–9, 101, 106,
   144; garrison 93–4; rubber
   cultivation 101–2, 144; Conference (1897) 127–8; present-
   day 144–5
Kuala Lumpur 15, 66; creation
   of 62–3; Residency 63, 66, 72,
   150; growth of 64, 109; improvement of 69–73, 114–16;
   rail link with Klang 73; social
   calendar 115–16; as capital of
   Federation 125–6; Conference

(1903) 131–2; present-day 146–
51, 159–60
Kudin, Tunku 34

Labuan 37
land administration 53, 108
Langat 25–6; 'Residency' 25, 28;
Innes as Collector and Magis-
trate 27–32
Larut 135–6; civil war in 3, 15,
23; Mentri of, confirmed as
ruler 5; Speedy as Acting
Assistant Resident 6, 23–4, 56;
Collector and Magistrate for
38; Chinese domination 56
Lela, Maharaja 16; hostility to
British intervention 12; and
murder of Birch 13–14, 22;
execution 22
Lias, M. Brau de Saint-Pol 87, 88,
93–4, 96–8
Light, Francis 1
Lister, Martin 75
Low, Sir Hugh: Perak Resident
36, 37–50, 76, 78, 87–9, 93–103,
113, 115, 142, 146, 150; earlier
career 37–8; his Residency at
Kuala Kangsa 38, 47–9, 87–9,
144; improvement of treasury
and revenue services 39–43; and
mining conditions 41–3; and
State Council 43, 65, 96–9; and
function 44; open house 44, 46;
pet apes 47–8; success 49–50,
102–3; and Maxwell 52, 59;
and *penghulus* 54, 55; botanical
interests 88–9, 101, 139; plantation agriculture 89, 100–2; and
abolition of slavery 94, 95–6,
98; economic reform 99–102;

introduction of rubber trees
101–2, 112; retirement 102–3
Lucas, Sir Charles 120, 121, 122

McNair, Major 15, 16, 17, 18, 19, 22
Mahmood, Raja 34
Malacca 2
Malay Civil Service 126, 147, 156
Malays: split among 3; antipathy
to Chinese 45, 55; literature
and folk-lore 58–9; and Malay
Civil Service 126–7
MARDI (Malaysian Research and
Development Institute) 154
Maxwell, Sir Peter Benson 17, 51
Maxwell, Sir William Edward
43, 142, 150; Assistant Resident, Kuala Kangsa 51–60, 92;
early career 52; concept of law
52–3; code of land regulations
53; improvement of judiciary
system 53–5; and authority of
penghulus 54–5; bias towards
Malays 55, 56; his Residency
at Taiping 56–7; study of
Malaysian literature and folk-
lore 58–9; antipathy to Swettenham 59–60, 105, 108, 111,
124; study of slavery 94;
Selangor Resident 104–5, 108–
9, 110–11, 114, 115, 119; reorganization of land administration 108; opposes plantation agriculture 117; Colonial
Secretary of Straits Settlements
122; Governor of Gold Coast 124
Maxwell Hill 111–12, 142
Meade, Sir Robert 21, 22, 44, 119
Mitchell, Sir Charles 121, 122, 131
motor-cars 136, 139–40